To David, partner in the travels

Acknowledgments

"Stone Wounds" was first printed in *Workshop 5: the Writing Process Revisited*, Thomas Newkirk, ed. (Heineman, 1994).

An earlier version of "Heart of Sand" was published as "Winter Dune" in *Traverse: Northern Michigan's Magazine* 22.9 (2003).

"The River Inside" was first published in *Dunes Review* 15.1 (2009).

"The Underpass" was published in *A River & Sound Review* no. 1 (2009), http://www.riverandsoundreview.org.

"Where Angels Are" was first published in *F Magazine* no. 8 (2009), http://f-magazine.org.

SOURCES:

Emily Dickinson's quote in "Wild Poem" is from *Final Harvest,* edited by Thomas H. Johnson (Back Bay Books, 1964).

The information about the Apache story is taken from *American Indian Myths and Legends,* selected and edited by Richard Erdoes and Alfonso Ortiz (Pantheon, 1985), and from *The Way of the Earth* by T. C. McLuhan (Touchstone, 1995).

Gary Snyder quotes taken from *The Gary Snyder Reader* (1999, Counterpoint Press).

Jim Harrison quote taken from "Modern Times," in *Saving Daylight* (2007, Copper Canyon Press).

John Steinbeck quotes taken from *Travels With Charley* (Viking, 1962).

James R. Akerman quotes taken from *Maps: Finding Our Place in the World,* edited by James R. Akerman and Robert W. Karrow Jr. (University of Chicago Press, 2007).

James Wright quote taken from "The Blessing," in *Selected Poems* (Farrar, Straus, and Giroux, 2005).

Stephen Vincent Benét quote taken from *John Brown's Body* (Rinehart Press, 1928).

DEEPEST GRATITUDE TO:
- David Early for believing in me so completely, for supporting the hours I have to spend away to do this work. Without you, pen doesn't touch paper.
- Annie Martin, editor, and the Wayne State University Press staff for their assistance and support; the WSUP anonymous

reviewers for their truly helpful suggestions on the final draft of this manuscript; Carrie Downes Teefey for her editing assistance; and Heidi Bell for copyediting.

- Betsy Eaton for her abiding friendship and for Flying Leap, the cottage in Maine where the first draft of this manuscript came together, and for the quiet support of her "Mainer" friends.

- Moonie and Chic Early, and to Justin Early, young Jake and Maddy Ruwitch, and the Early family for allowing the long mornings in Fred's House on the shore of the Huzzah River in Missouri to begin the first major revision of this manuscript.

- Gilbert Sellers and family for the tour of the Gilbert cemetery.

- Jackie McClure for the Mount Rainier hike and for her friendship.

- Natalie Bakapoulis for an astute reading of "Finding (My) America."

- Marijo and John Bakker for the New York Trip.

- Anne de Mare and Kirsten Kelly, filmmakers of *Asparagus: Stalking the American Life.*

- Marijo Bakker and Patti and Ian Harpe for the trip to Eleven Mile River Canyon.

- Keith Taylor and Richard Tillinghast for inspiration for this book, particularly the essay, "Finding Cochise," and for the amazing Bear River Writers' Conference

- Joe VanderMeulen for advice on the alvar.

- The Michigan Library Association, especially Judith Moore and Kim Laird, for the means to make the library tour. And to the librarians.

- My colleagues at Interlochen Arts Academy and most especially Michael Delp, Jack Driscoll, Lesley Tye, Mika Perrine, Teresa Scollon, Therese Zielinski; and to the administration, especially President Jeffrey Kimpton and Vice President for Education Tim Wade, for supporting my travel for the school, particularly for the trip to Santa Monica.

- Writers at Solstice Conference at Pine Manor College, especially Meg Kearney and Tanya Whiton.

- The circle of friends, near and far, who give me courage: Norm and Mimi Wheeler, Bronwyn Jones and Joe Vander-Muelen, Jeanette Mason, Pauline Tyer, Judy Reinhardt and Jim Schwantes, Cre Woodard and Mark Ringlever, Carlene and Geoff Peregrine, Ruthie Nathan, David and Sharon Hendricks, Jack Gyr and Dianne Navarro, Patty McNair and Phillip Hartigan, Dana McConnell and Walter Elder, and my young friends who set an example for me every day in their activism: Jacob Wheeler and Sarah Eichberger, Julia Wheeler and Martin Ludden, Annie Oberschulte and Emerson Hilton.

- Members of Michigan Writers, particularly Aaron and Mary Kay Stander, Michael Callahan, Ann Bardens, Heather Shaw, Bill Corbett, Marcy Branski, Denise Baker, Fleda Brown, Todd Mercer, Mardi Link, Michael Sheehan, Duncan Sprattmoran, Anne Noble, Holly Spaulding, Leigh Fairey and many others in that essential circle.

- All of my students who continue to teach me.

American muse, whose strong and diverse heart
So many men have tried to understand
But only made it smaller with their art,
Because you are as various as your land. . . .

I only bring a cup of silver air,
Yet, in your casualness, receive it there.

Stephen Vincent Benét

Warming the Flue

Tucked as it is in a Michigan woods thick with tall maple and ash, the Think House eddies with chill in winter, and remains too-cool and shaded in the summer.

So I build a fire in the woodstove.

A decade ago in Leelanau County, my David and I built by hand this sixteen-by-twenty cabin out of mostly recycled, damaged, or deeply discounted goods. As a result, each autumn we seal leaky windows with plastic and stuff insulation strips around the eternally peeling though still partly brilliant red door. The small black Jotel perches in the corner—inadequate against drafts—and dusty pine bookcases filled to bending line the walls—doing double duty as insulation when the cold comes on. A butcher-block table faces the insect-spotted window; a second-hand desk holds a newer computer; a school chair leans toward the woodstove. Here are a Depression-era rocker; three dictionaries—two unabridged, one belonging to my grandmother; and more books—revealing an obsession with having them as much as with reading.

I wad newspaper into rough coils and place them side by side in the chamber. I pile shards of pine and scrap walnut on the wasted news, crisscrossing them like highways on a map. Then I realize it's so cold that I have to warm the flue before I start the fire. I roll a full sheet of newspaper into a long crinkled tube. I light one end with a wooden match, hold it into the firebox, seeking that small invisible place where a hint of draft should pull. I sit back on my heels.

In this room, wild turkey feathers tuck into cracks, lake stones rest on sills, Petoskey fossils serve as doorstops. The place is rough on all its edges, messy with piles, and it lacks plumbing—though the electricity works most of the time. It is too quiet—except for wind, the voice that always enters this place.

Still.

Here is the place where the stories and poems take root. But even before that, where does the process begin? At what point is the imagination sparked? Just as there must be fuel to warm the cold stove's firebox, there must be inspiration for the imagination to warm.

Will the fire take? I wait in the cold. Sometimes when the chimney is too cold, the warm smoke is trapped and back-puffs, filling the cluttered room. Then there is only coughing and ugly haze.

I've worked in this room for years, fired this stove every cold day that needed warming. I know the ways of this stove I bend to; I also know how my thinking goes. It doesn't always work, this attempted combustion of air and tinder—or its parallel of imagination and language. The writing doesn't come from nowhere. Other routes, like a tube of flaming paper to channel fire and warm the flue, must warm the mind. The fuel of travel, the experience of other places and their people inspire me.

For me, this desire to seek out new places is not simple; despite an innate curiosity, I love home and isolation. Solitude. The chill of the Think House, the wind against it. In contrast, the intensity of New York City unnerves me, the Mexican border disturbs me, Culebra's wild surf shakes me. Always I feel uncertain and often lonely opening the door on fresh territory, following new routes away from old roots. It feels blank and anxiety-ridden, and, yes, I thrive on it. I pack.

The tube of old news flutters, unwilling. I bend to it. Fire grows from fire, small to large. But nothing happens without the air, the oxygen drawing across it to feed it. I blow a little.

Lately I have been thinking about how discrete places, and perhaps an entire country, might become placeless. No, not placeless, for that is more or less impossible, but how places might lose their individuality, and in turn lose their meaning. I sense the disquiet, the loss of place that may be happening in my America. Will we one day alter Pete Seeger's melancholy anthem: *where have all the places gone?*

Are they still out there—places where meaning and geography and people are linked so closely they make the stories that give us identity, that make us a people? We can still find them, can't we?

I imagine the inside of the chimney, the clash of the warm air I have created against the cold air still holding in the upper regions of the pipe. Fire, too, has this restlessness in its nature, the built-in imperative to move into unexplored space, to taste new air.

The tubed flame, held into the firebox like food for a shy pet, suddenly shifts, lifts, is accepted at last. With sudden decision, the flame plumes up, and its drifting smoke is routed all at once, a poof into the flue and the pipe, to the open, its heat warming the cold chimney, warming interior chambers with its draw, preparing it for fire.

Metaphor arrives, its small miracle puffing.

I am rooted in place in my Think House with its warming stove. I follow routes of place out into the open. But I also root out places—as the farmer pulls plants to understand growth—and I root as a baby does, paradoxically seeking the nourishment from not a mother but from places all over the country, the mother country.

Through the writing, I enter still another form of rooting out, of making and remaking these places in language, in words that seek to fire the imagination of others. Place-making. And in reimagining the faraway places here at home, I root out, through my own mother tongue, what place might mean, not simply a specific place, but the idea and meaning of place. Place-meaning. And in this process, discovering, thinking, and writing, rooting out place and places in my America, feeding the fire, my anxiety eases. A kind of compassion comes.

My country 'tis of thee. . .

Stone Wounds

Mount Cardigan, New Hampshire

When I break the tree line and look up to the crest, I am suddenly dizzy. I stop, resting against the slabs of granite that grace New Hampshire's Mount Cardigan. That is when I notice the quartz for the first time. The dark granite runs with veins of lighter quartz, long lines crossing and crisscrossing this rock like a child's script, teasing some words or a story just to the edge of recognition—a mystery, almost a meaning. I hear in the abrupt wind some question I do not understand. Then I remember.

The stone stories slip back to me. Stones are threaded in me as this mountain is threaded with quartz, but like the shadow that lace casts, the pattern is dark, the holes filled with light. I begin to climb again, turning my mind away from my anxiety,

making an odd preparation to reach the crest: I remember that
stones have marked graves for a long time. That, and Isaac.

Of the huge tract of fields, swamp, and pasture that graced
the Michigan farm where I grew up, my siblings and I were
forbidden from playing on only one acre of untilled hillside
north of our asparagus fields. An odd Eden. Chief Isaac Bat-
tice, the man who would later tell me the story, spoke to my
father, explained that two generations before my father's father bought the farm, it had been part of treaty land. On the
southwest slope of this hill lay a tribal cemetery, probably the
first one established in Oceana County after the mission and
settlement era. My father agreed to Isaac's request that the
cemetery be left alone. Even we who roamed everywhere over
the hills were told not play there. Thus, as defiance overcomes
any rule, it became one of our favorite haunts. If ever wooden
crosses marked anything, we made them buttresses for our
forts; we ransacked the remnants of a fence to make toy guns.

On some level, my father understood the ramifications that
his farm, and the entire county, had likely been part of one
of the many betrayed treaties, but we children missed entirely
the contract of reverence and guilt my father held with Isaac
regarding this heritage. It shames me to say our childhood in-
vasion of the place was what we did simply because it was
banned, and my father was too caught in the turning gears of
farming to pay notice past his initial agreement. And if Isaac
saw, he said nothing further.

Isaac was one of the few members of the local Pottawattamie tribe who had not scattered but who still inhabited what
we called Shanty Town, a few small, battered shacks down by
the big spring. My father kept an eye out for him hitchhiking,
and my mother drove down after bad winter storms to see that

he was still alive. That was the extent of it. I used to stare at the way he walked, an odd gait that must have covered terrible arthritis. I didn't understand what it meant that he was "Indian."

Years later, during the growing consciousness of the sixties, I sat in Isaac's shack, intent on an interview with him. Through my youth, I had developed an association with the man. Whether he sensed my interest in him or if he was friendly to me simply because I was the oldest of my father's children, he always smiled broadly at me and made a point of offering conversation when he came to the house, or when our family had cause to visit the spring. I liked him, and while I did not seek him out particularly, these accidental encounters seemed to please both of us. Over time, my childhood interest in American Indian lore grew, and that interest, coupled with the national attention caused by Wounded Knee in 1973, spurred an interest in cultural anthropology. My final paper for one of my college courses was to be about Isaac.

My so-called raised consciousness didn't reveal my own unexamined ethnocentrism. From a more developed perspective, this interview would be yet another version of co-opting the culture of native people. But I merely felt proud of this connection to him, and when I asked to interview him about his childhood and his time in the "boarding schools" where so many Indians were orphaned, he seemed happy to speak to me. He shared his life easily, a born storyteller. Ironically, in that long past time, he made me feel that speaking to me was an honor. Too late, I know the honor was mine.

We sat on run-down straight-backed chairs in the single front room that served as bedroom and living room. We shared a bottle of cheap wine. He stood near the smoking oil furnace, picking out old church hymns on a three-stringed fiddle in a room that became suffocatingly warm. Weather was

blowing up from the lake. Thunder entered the room, nour-
ishing the atmosphere of hazy air with the drum of storm.
Distant heat lightning flashed through dirty windows. From
any other view, the scene might have been ominous, but I felt
only a passionate interest in his words. I bent to my notebook
and pencil, my questions and follow-up. I did not see the harm
or loss; I merely heard the man's voice, warm and resonant.
He gave me a gift I knew was important but not exactly how.
He told me the stone story. I have no tape recording of it, and
the rough notes have long since been lost, but I remember the
story like this:

Before time began, the People fought a great battle. The
battle raged over the whole world, and the greatest warriors,
warriors with the best skills, finest weapons, and fastest bodies
fought in this battle. The battle raged on and on over land and
time. The warriors fought to the death. And at last, after much
time had passed, they all killed each other. But their battle was
so great that when they died, these warriors turned to great
dark stones marked by lines of lighter horizontal color, like
layers between a cake. Isaac told me how to know the warrior
stones.

Later, I was to learn that the legend held such strength that
the first missionaries who came to Michigan's coast allowed
the Pottawattamie to place these striated rocks in the first
Christian cemeteries, where the mythic warriors could be honored with the newly dead. But after the second wave, when the
missionaries built the Saint Joseph Mission with its new Indian
cemetery, the priests placed the rocks outside the boundaries
of the cemetery and forbade the Pottawattamie from touching
them because the stones represented a pagan practice. Isaac
told me the stones disappeared. Then he laughed and said that
at night the tribe moved them into another older cemetery

that would no longer be used. A cemetery the priests would forget.

Isaac showed me this older cemetery, on a wooded hillside in Elbridge Township. Overgrown, no crosses and few gravestones. One plaque did claim to mark the grave of Chief Cobmoosa (or, as we in Northern Michigan call him, "Cobmoosie"), the man who was supposed to have hidden the gold when tribal lands were sold to the government. Here also stood warrior stones shaped like trolls, three to five feet high, some squat, some slim, many tilted with vine. Through the dark rock, slim horizontal lines of a lighter granite or quartz ran like veins. Isaac touched the lines, reminding me, "These are how you will know."

The story, despite the vagaries of time and memory, has stayed with me. Thousands of miles from my Great Lakes homeland, I touch rock on an old mountain in New Hampshire—granite streaked with foam from Earth's great cooldown. However, geology does not stun me as much as legend, the sudden thought: *How huge, how magnificent were these warriors. Here the battle was so great and fought so hard, warriors died above clouds and became crests of mountains.*

My father's huge hands grapple with the wheel of the pickup as he swings onto a two-track bordering the asparagus field. It is a spring Saturday and my niece, Brooke's, eighth birthday. I am home, a rare visit, and with my sister, Marijo, and our father, we are in charge of seven grandchildren—Marijo's three, and two boys from each of my brothers. The "silly seven" have piled into the truck bed, except for Brooke, who rides with us in the cab.

"Why are we going here?" she asks as Dad drives deeper into the farm hills.

"We're looking for an old cemetery," Marijo explains.

"How come?" Brooke asks.

"We want to see if we can still find it."

"But why?" Brooke insists.

"People are buried there."

"Can we really find it?"

"We don't know. We used to play there," I sigh. "But we beat it up pretty bad when we were your age. There may be nothing left."

I am remembering the remnants of structures that were even then pocked with weather and rot.

Dad shakes his head. Isaac has recently died. In the elegiac stories following his death, we have told my father about our childhood wildness in the cemetery. And perhaps because of his own age and legacy, my father is remembering his long-ago promise. He wants to make amends by making sure this generation remembers better.

"Will there be ghosts?" Brooke's voice, unsure. Marijo hugs her only daughter.

"No, Brooke, we want to stake it so you will all know where it is," Marijo explains.

"Nothing to be afraid of." This, my dad's voice. "We just want to remember."

"Why do we want to remember?"

"It's a sacred thing," he rumbles softly, sounding remarkably like an old chief I once knew.

His softened ambitions, his slow comprehension of the historical betrayal, and of course Isaac's death have touched my father. He better understands what he understood only superficially as a younger man. He has made a plan about how to teach his grandkids.

We follow the two-track north to its end and park the truck

at the bottom of a slope that leads to a hilltop ridge. The ridge is the north boundary of the farm, and the cemetery lies just within that boundary, near the crest of the ridge. Since this particular acreage has always been harsh land to till, the field has this year been left fallow in preparation for planting pine trees next year. We will have to walk the final hundred yards up the slope through rough grasses and short scrub.

My father pulls out the shovel and four long iron stakes. The kids tumble out like puppies, bumping into each other, piling onto the land. Marijo calls them before they spread too far, and they come back, tethered to her voice. Dad squats on his heels, knees splayed a little, elbows resting on his knees, huge hands hovering over air and sand, making an odd blessing. His voice is quieter than usual as he tells the kids what we are doing. "We're looking for an old cemetery where some people are buried. We're going to mark it. You kids must promise never to till this land." Then he tells them about Isaac and the Pottawattamie and the farm. He talks a bit more about what the word *sacred* means.

Marijo takes up the narrative. "We want you all to know where it is so you can help each other remember."

I realize the incongruity of taking seven white children to the site of an old Indian cemetery, so that when they own the land, they will remember not to till it.

Near the crest, a mountain breeze springs up. I move across steep rocks, invigorated by the coolness and pushed forward by my memory of a story. Stories understand what we don't. They offer reasons for the things we have no reasons for; they calm fears; they connect people to each other and to places in unexpected ways. Perhaps stories come into being because we need them. Certainly, stories may have many meanings, and new meanings unfold as our view of the world changes. Maybe stories give up particular secrets only when we are ready to know them. The fear I experienced while climbing begins to fade as I realize I am caught in a lace made of the veins running through rock, the lines of a story about stone, the lines drawn around a plot of land on a hillside. I begin to imagine what it will be like to step through the lace into the light.

We trudge the hillside, heading north, the silly seven spreading before and behind us. For them, this is still an adventure with their grandpa and their aunts, and the unruly south-facing hillside does not yet have a reference point. They climb the slope for the joy of it; it is the adults who have reason to slow, look for landmarks—the distant road, the shadow of former fields—to examine the rolling contours of this hillside more closely. We approach the crest. I wonder, as I push through low-growing sumac, if it will be hard to find.

I needn't have worried.

Dad and Marijo find the south edge of the cemetery almost immediately. It ends abruptly on the brow where we encounter a raised edge that runs for the distance of half an acre—as though a fenceline had once run its course there. I ask Dad if he knows what created the ridge. "The earliest farmers who didn't till this acre plowed right up against its boundary. Over generations, their own fields began to wash away. But in here, the cemetery grasses anchored the topsoil in place." We walk the ridge. On the inside of this boundary, wild grapes grow dense, coiled into a dark tangle over which the kids trip, whining that these woods are "boogie trapped." Once inside this boundary, inside what would have been the cemetery, we cross also into more dense vegetation. Indeed, it is returning to the wild. The scrub forest thickens with saplings on which the kids swing.

Marijo and Dad and I follow the south edge, looking for a clue to the perpendicular boundary that will give us then one corner and two sides to the plot. We find the rotted wrist of a cedar pole. The second corner discovered, but now the plot's raised edge has faded. Finally, by digging on a parallel line to the first ridge, our hands touch on a line of barbed wire rusted to the color of dried blood, embedded in leaf mold. It guides us to the third corner. There, we find a large stone, too large to be an accident. It is a marker stone, smooth and round as a giant's knee bone. I realize how difficult it must have been to get it there. We estimate where the last leg of the square might lie and walk along it. Zach, the oldest boy, discovers the last corner. He digs until he finds termite dust ten or twelve inches below the surface, wood turned into red powder, evidence of the cedar post that once stood here.

As we discover each corner, my father drives a stake. The children, wild with wind and fascination, swarm into ritual spontaneously as we drive the last one. They tumble against my father, grabbing the stake, swinging on this new boundary marker. Suddenly he announces, "Kids, we're gonna walk the boundary again, all the way around, so you won't forget." What happens is that at each corner each child places a small hand around the stake and holds it. No words are spoken but a vow occurs—never forget to respect this sacred place. We walk this small plot, and at every corner seven children and two sisters and their father take hold, and iron vibrates as a new generation promises not only to honor the boundaries by not tilling the property, but also not to invade a place made sacred by the bodies once placed there and now forgotten. On the third corner, where the bone-stone lies, my father has driven the stake outside the line so that now the stone rests within the cemetery. The children put their hands on the stake, but they also touch the stone, brushing away dirt as they climb over it.

On the way down, Brooke hangs back, takes her grandfather's hand, and says, "This sure was a funny birthday present, Grandpa."

I take the last strides, and at the brink of Mount Cardigan, the wind and view bring a final clarity. I look around at this fine old mountain warrior, and I feel nothing of the conqueror, more the trespasser, but I am here. I bend down, and with my hands I touch a wide line of running quartz. I walk over the crest, more reverent than I ever have been in church, awed at these marks left by weapons I cannot imagine, tracing a web of scars that never heals, to honor the existence of death and to acknowledge that stone is the closest thing to eternity we know.

The lines identified the stones as warriors. The warriors could not live to sing their exploits but their wounds mark the land forever. I lie down on the rock. Isaac never told me if the warriors were honorable, if theirs was a noble cause; he only told me that it happened, how to know and remember. If the story were to carry a lesson, perhaps it reminds us to be tenacious, to fight to the death; perhaps it reminds us to keep the peace, that the great battle has already been fought, and we need fight no more. But I think meaning rests in the nature of story itself, in the way we make story to answer great questions and in how good stories last because they mean many things.

I believe, because of this new ritual, my brothers' and sister's children will remember better than we did to respect the cemetery, not to till an acre of land marked by a stone, bones, and four iron stakes. Perhaps they will even tell the story of seven children taken by two sisters and their father to drive stakes on a southwest hillside. If we are very lucky, the story will run ahead of us for as long as these wounds and this story have run. Because these lines (on the stone and in the field and on the page and now in your mind) are more than a story to trace with your fingertips: they are the open places, the wounds of making and remaking meaning.

Today I have climbed a warrior so great that I lie down in the rocklight of a story. My body rests parallel to a wound in stone that is like blood running forever, stilled in Isaac's tale. I fall asleep here in light and wind, knowing the great warrior on which I sleep is protected by and linked to the iron stake of story and the stone of memory.

Wild Poem

Mount Rainier, Washington

I was raised in what's called "low country," country that is permeated by horizontals: wide meandering rivers, seeping wetlands, flatland fields, the perfect horizon of the Great Lakes. Even the bowls of our thousands of inland lakes are that, bowl-like, filled by gravity with freshwater sweetness that draws the eye across distances, but not up. Low country. It is a relative description, for we do have rolling hills and high dunes of sand that sport places of steepness, and the Upper Peninsula's great mineral fault line forced up a low range of fairly impressive mountains. But they are still that—low—compared to the Western Rockies. Mountains, especially big mountains with their righteous verticality, are news to me. Their steeply diagonal slopes pull the eye up and up again to points that pierce clouds. A mountain's slopes and soaring lofts seem to defy gravity, and that majestic rock-hard upward existence leaves me with a strange vertigo. This mountain idea is not so much too big as too tall. Even the sky bows and serves.

This is how to make peace with such stature.

This is how to find rest in elevation.

What I learn is that hiking a big mountain is honor and privilege, but its other grace is finding a place within a place, a place interior and nearly horizontal to contrast with the mountain's omnipresent height.

But you cannot find these places without a guide.

Post grad school. For several years, I slept little and studied hard, and now my head rings with an academic din of language that I cannot silence. I have handed in the bound document, undergone the final presentation, read aloud to a hundred people, said good-bye to my advisors and taken on a new job where I have self-promoted, self-marketed, and become totally self-absorbed. Now, insomnia, back spasms, headaches, bronchitis, moodiness. More insomnia. I can't write, not poems or stories, not even a scrap of a play—which was the purpose of all this education. Even my beloved David, with his kind attention, cannot resolve this.

He does what good men do; he lets me go to someone who can offer refuge. It is a long plan and a longer flight to the small town outside of Seattle, but I have come to Jackie, my friend who completed her degree the year before, who writes the trajectory of birds and things that swim, writes the story of creatures who live in places we cannot imagine unless some wise being can take us there. She can name a thousand plants—or so it seems to me, having heard her walk an ordinary street and rattle off every weed and grass and flower in view, as though she were speaking to them.

Sitting in her sun-and-shadow kitchen, she lets me churn through the academic gossip that has been dammed inside me for months, how this writer did that thing to her manuscript, how this professor massacred that paper, which advisor said what to whom about whoever's thesis and where it will get published. All of it is petty complaint and petulant brag, and it always comes back to me. I have become an egocentric automaton, a robotic creature out of sync with its natural mechanics, and even the words I love are not my own, but the vocabulary of the literary critics. I want to write new and wild poems, but writing feels *like squeezing dried fruit,* I tell her. I can't hear even a line for the ruckus in my head.

She pours tea and listens. When, like some worn-out wind up toy, I slump over the pretty tablecloth and take a long breath, preparing to launch again, she pulls out a hiking book and flips pages.

"Mount Rainier . . ." she says softly.

Still babbling, I help her load the backpacks.

We park at a deep mountain lake so clear that we can see the cross-hatching of deadwood thirty feet below the surface. We start early, shouldering day packs, checking the Paradise Trail postings, orienting to weight and stride. At first, a wide curve of trail along a talus slope through young hemlock and cedar, but then we enter the interior—great hemlocks rising, weaving their own thick canopy, towering over an understory of fern. The path narrows, drops more steeply on one side. When I look out through the near tree trunks, I am looking into what Jackie calls the *overstory of evergreens.* The words understory and overstory hum a little in my head—a first small shift.

My nickname for Jackie is Longstrider for the obvious reason that she is tall and long-legged. She is a sister-spirit, mainly
because we have laughed so hard together that we have each
other's gasping. We roomed together every semester at God-
dard College until she graduated, and though we see each
other only every few years, we have the kind of friendship that
will remain an oasis even in abeyance.

Her straight back is my sturdy flag, my way of seeing where
I have to go. She is ahead on the trail that will take us as high
as we can get in one day's walk. It is her steady—never ag-
gressive—pace that keeps my bad back and less well-toned legs
from cramping. It is she who knows the path, she who leads
me into each moss-covered moment, onto the narrow stone
shelves, over the rough-shod bridges under which melted
snow roils down the rocky creekbeds. The river waters here
are as green as you would expect to find in the Caribbean but
retain a true cold all year. Their soft color originates from the
silt that washes down with the melt. All the long run to the Pacific, these mountain rivers collect microscopic granules, tiny
green crystals in multitudes of stars, tinting the water a deceptive turquoise, a minty paleness to contrast with the coming-
down-hard chaos of a mountain river.

The path rises, switches back and roughens as we climb.
It softens only in places where needles blanket the ground,
and then it hardens again in scabbed rock. We lose it entirely
where a rockslide has buried it, and we scramble across this
stony bubble of rocks, leaning sideways against the mountain,
searching for the point where the path slides out from under
on the other side. Though we are here in the season when this
western slope is relatively dry, the rockslide warns us that the
mountain contains secrets waiting to reveal themselves in high

drama. Mount St. Helens is not so far away, and its proximity reminds us to respect the smaller restlessness of these elder rocks. A mountain is no eternally sleeping giant, but alive with lettings-go.

To hike even a short way up a mountainside is to touch height, the overriding sloop of rock, but it is also to touch a hearth of flora. Here are more hemlock, Douglas fir, and young western red cedar, comparatively small but decades old. The air stills between the canopy and the elegant ferns, the subtle mosses. Mist is less mist than haze. We are close to the temperate rain forests, the only ones in our nation, and even here in the higher climes, there is that echo of laden air. Always, the breath of the walk alternates warm to cool. Warm, cool, warm, cool, warmcoolwarmwarm—I thrust my hand into ferns where a chill holds like the undersurface of a pool. Cool.

A side trail, a less-traveled path. Cross a rough bridge, climb the stone steps, follow a ridge where the light warms as trees thin. Rougher scrambling—then a sudden, quick openness, a water roar so acute, it startles. We cannot see the mountain above us. Rather, overwhelming the view, a high wide bluff from which liquid silks rocket down a gorge of cliffs and boulders, pools and precipices. No peaceful moment here, but an uproar so loud we can't hear words, can barely think in the presence of a river blasting whole off the mountain, shredding in its fall into sheets and tubes of foam, thinning to hard rain that strikes the rocks just above us, splays open, bounces to our feet where it swirls, thrilled, and then shouts its way beyond and down, wilded by mountain. Because of this fortissimo of river, we don't speak much, and as I drop my backpack, I realize I have little to say anyway, my internal chatter finally drowned out by falling water.

We stop here, on the rock shelves overlooking the down-driven river, to rest and eat. Jackie has brought meatless sandwiches, fruit, precious water. We let the spray mist our hair. Finally, damp but refreshed, we ease on our packs and return to the path. Shortly, we angle upward, switch back, angle up again for . . . how many miles? Hours pass. Though I am tired, my legs are steady with the work. My back twinges but does not spasm. The day heats up as we climb into higher elevations, and slim light shafts through the verticality of trees. My ragged breathing becomes reliable. Count these steps: *one, two, three;* count these breaths: *four, five, six.*

A thousand breaths. Ten thousand steps.

I do not at first notice the leveling off, the shift from the intense diagonal of the slopes to an almost-though-not-quite horizontal. It is as though some high vertical gate has been lowered before us, pivoting gently downward as we walk from one ecosystem to another. And being the poet she is, Jackie does not announce this change of plane. She holds off as long as she can, creating the turn, a trope. After the elegance of tall trees, these are short, matted. Tree clumps. Troll-like. She gives me no words, but I will eventually learn the one for this—*krumholz.* Crooked wood. I think at first that their tops have been harvested. Now they have sprouted these low branches that twist together in gnarled clumps and lean in one direction like tattered flags. But she tells me this is what the mountain winter does—*blows away their tops.* I think of Emily Dickinson's words about a good poem taking off the top of one's head. Without their tops, they grow close to the surface of the mountain, ducking under wind. Jackie points out their *skirts,* the prostrate circle of roots that cling even in this thin layer of humble soil.

A wind to blow away your top, your crown, your reaching

ambition for sun.

The tree line, she says, indicating this is where the tall trees stop growing, where the ecosystem shifts, a transition.

Then the trees disappear, giving way to a land covered by grasses.

No, not grasses.

Pink, yellow, and white drifts of flowers burst through a wash of grasses and gray, lichen-covered stones.

A field?

She smiles, gives me the title for this wild poem.

Alpine Meadow.

A meadow.

Then, words so lush and gorgeous I roll the sounds in my mouth like sweets. *Carex, partridgefoot, huckleberry, campion, spreading phlox, paintbrush, cinquefoil, mountain heather.*

She tells me this is a *snowbed community.*

Snowbed?

For months, undercover of snow, tiny perennials wait and wait and wait for winter to recede, and when it does, often in one quick-drying day, using what little moisture is left, they bloom in bright, eye-bursting palettes so that insects will love them to death. In a mere handful of days these plants must bloom, be ravished in pollination, make seed, burst their seed-pods, and go dormant before the snow flies again, which is always soon. They have a brief past, a briefer future. But today time stretches out on both sides, buzzing with . . . what?

Jackie says, *Listen.*

I heard a fly buzz . . .

Not one fly, but hundreds—the meadow is a song, a chorus of flies. And not just flies, but deep-throated bees and small beetles with luscious carapaces of color and gnats and winged things neither of us can name. Jackie shows me plants that

grow fine hairs all over themselves to serve as garb, an outer-
wear of insulation, and inside these matted interlacings, as hiding places for bugs. Oh, here is the meadow's chamber suite,
written in the subtle hum of wings, in the soft litanies of pollination, in this ground-loving clump of blooms, all rustling
over the contours of slopes so often unkind.

We step carefully along the narrow trail, drinking in the
high-dry notes of sweetness, the meadow world's saturnalia of
survival. In the distance, a doglike body and tail flash into the
scrub. Coyote? Fox? Is she hunting, or like us, has she come to
the one place where the mountain's singular gentling allows it,
as the poet James Wright said, to *break into blossom*.

Finally, the mountain shifts again, exerts its more severe nature, and after this fecund display, rises again, barren. Pocked
with patchy grasses, small strands of lichen, rocks slab and
scrabble up the slopes as they steepen—and now the mountain is close, so close there can be no argument. Line drawn.
There is no soil, little moisture, and the air thins harshly. Nothing much grows above this point. It is now all altitude. It is the
mountain's boundary and a warning to casual day hikers like
us, and we turn back to meadow, back into the shallow-valley
of bees and flies. We find a broad rock, sit and lean into it. The
sun dries our sweat. We rest in that warm air that flirts with
cool, in a humming moment between past and future. I think
Jackie sleeps.

I listen for a long time to this thing that is all color and no
words, this most tenacious ecosystem, designed to call the
smallest wings to the smallest colored stars. Here on the face
of the mountain, Jackie has given me a waterfall to erase the
buzz that hurts, and in the silence that formed she asked me
to listen to the skirted roots, the hairy interiors, to hear instead the smallest buzzing flies. "I heard a fly buzz—when I

died—" Dickinson's line continues. Short life meets short life
and thrives between snowmelt and freezing snow.

I suspect I will never completely escape self-consciousness,
the gummy self-centeredness of the ego, but here in an alpine
meadow, in this low place secreted within the high drama of
mountain, a letting go, a small death that brings welcome relief. Contradiction and gift. While the mountain rises above us
in its implacable work of height and grandness, sleep comes, a
low country of rest with its mixed hum of bees and sun seeping into me from the rock, my first wild poem.

Long, long ago, the earth was made. Then the One Who Made the Earth also planned for each person to have a piece of land that he could live on and call his own. Our people were living in one such place but they didn't like that particular spot. So the One Who Made the Earth told them to move to a new location, and when they did, they slept well, and liked it and lived in a good way.   *Apache tale*

Finding Cochise

Cochise Stronghold, Arizona

I should go back. I am way too deep into these mountains, and I am a stranger to them, and I am off trail. But the rock of the Dragoons has the scent of dust and spirit that I am drawn to like arrow to prey, that sunset scent of destiny or accident—I'm not sure which. These mountains are the pale red of blood washed not quite successfully from a white shirt. They are shaped of soft karsts that shear off in boulder-sized chunks, stacked palisades that look like bulging rolls of dough upended on some giant's table. There are crevasses and couloirs and small sheltered alcoves where someone could hide, and long, winding canyons with spirit rivers that come and go with rainy and dry seasons. They are not high mountains but rugged and stubborn and tainted with the scarlet palette of deception and secrets. There are places inside places in this mountain maze, shadows within shadows of peaks and spires, ideal for mystics and renegades.

Because the trail has been washed out in early winter storms, I scramble up the now-dry creek bed. Those washes carved away the river bottom, leaving huge stones and deadfall. Now, months later, I have to leap giant spiders of brittle mesquite jettisoned onto the bed by drought. I clip another ten rock-laden yards, only half-looking for the intersecting trail, which is supposed to cross this dry bed. I want to get to the crest, where I am sure the moraines and ridges will tell me where to find him.

David grunts as he follows, climbing through yucca scrub below me. Stumbling into sudden gloom, I look up to see the late-day rush, rust colored, across the mountain ridge and toothy peaks. The terrain's rare diction, silent and alkaline, announces that I do not belong here. I am pampered. I have expensive hiking boots, and I am running stupidly low on water. The Apache belonged here, and I am not of them. Or rather, the N'de, the Apache name for themselves. *Apache* meant enemy, a name given by another tribe.

David calls up from fifty feet down, that soft-voiced way he says my name when he has to ask something that he knows I will want, in my own equally quiet way, to defy.

"Anne-Marie . . ."

My name couples with our rough breaths, slips out of purpose toward the heights facing us. Even as softly as David speaks, an almost-echo trips into something stony and rebellious. I point to a series of dark eyes along the ridge.

"There are caves in those ridges."

I can hear the man-sigh that is his loudest act of impatience toward me. "The path crosses down here."

I look up, trying to assess the climb, time and distance, but the red rock is turning maroon. *Old blood,* my tracking father would say, and I feel the mystery of what is cave and what is simply shadow harden and close itself off. A lone raven in a near peak chucks his scold our way: *Get out of here.* The shadows sliver, everywhere longer through the cactus and scrub, and when I glance back, I can barely make out the short precipice and corner of the cistern, landmark for the path that will take us down.

David waits there, shifting the day toward good sense.

But I want to stay here. Because it is here in the Dragoon Mountains that Cochise and his last followers, nearly one thousand of them, came to hide. From here he ran raids, kept his warriors, died and was buried, and his burial place is kept secret by these rocks, by these mountains. And I have the audacity to be looking for his grave. Or to imagine that I am. Or to put it more precisely, I want to find him, spirit or otherwise, to fulfill the dream—half bravado, half longing heart, all wish—that I made early that morning, before the police cars and the search, *I want to find Cochise.*

As a child my male heroes were Roy Rogers, because he sang "Happy Trails," the Lone Ranger and Tonto, for reasons I can't remember, and my secret hero, Cochise, because I saw a movie in which he appeared in all the ways we would now perceive as politically incorrect—the Noble Savage, the Good Indian, the one who fought for justice and for a little while won, but inevitably lost, and *wasn't that romantic, the way he went down, disappearing like that?* It was among those sixties movies supposedly intended to raise our consciousness about American Indian history but that mostly manipulated us, native people included, into unexamined, blind admiration.

Of course, as an adult, I know it's more complicated. Cochise, depending on your perspective, was a bloodthirsty villain of the worst kind or a great leader and avenger who, after the death of Mangas Coloradas, led the Apache bands that continued to fight for their Southwest territories before being overcome. By all accounts, he was visionary; there are stories of the way he could garner loyalty, the way he led his people. He also became, over time, as ruthlessly cruel as those bitter captains of the U.S. military, who time and again tried to exterminate him and his people.

When David and I picked Cochise County, Arizona, for our first-ever vacation away from the Great Lakes, it was presumably to go to a warm place during the season when we Michiganders are most tired of winter, to explore a region dramatically different from the upper Midwest but not too expensive. But I had read the guidebooks. I knew the history. Cochise was there.

A highway intersection in Arizona, out on the desert floor, surrounded by flat, pocked land, will come at you for a long time. We are driving, still miles away from the Cochise Stronghold and the mountain hike we have planned. We are an ordinary couple approaching middle age, in the middle of careers, but able at last to get away, to be easy with each other in motion— the long mating worn smooth—able to rent a car without guilt and drive, speeding even, in short sleeves with the windows down into a desert so warm and foreign we feel giddy. We sweat and the moisture is immediately drawn into the not unpleasantly dry air, and our skin is glazed with a talc of juniper scent. There is the persistent note of heat singing under too-clear morning air. Highway 191, a single thread of gray, corners its way north of the border from Douglas through the

desert all the way to the state's northern line and beyond. But
we will turn off at the road to the Dragoons and the Stronghold and the trails.

The desert with its pale browns and tufts of yellowed grass
stretches all around us in what my rolling-hills farm folk would
have called flat land, saying it as one word. *Flatland*. Here, even
the sky seems flat, a long stretch of thin blue muscle reaching
for the horizon, that foil of heat shimmering so far away we
finally have to stop looking toward it to stop the shifting sense
that *something* is out there. I stare at the low pin oaks, at ir-
rigation ditches running soupily east and west, to the sides of
the highway littered with grass-matted debris—hubcaps, old
plows, pickup bodies without wheels or even axles, all of it
desiccated to the quality of insect carapaces. We notice the
low stucco houses without yards, or rather with gravel yards,
and the occasional bright flowerpot, and then, beyond, the
sand so light it rises like mist, or sometimes a field of something we cannot name, all of that leaning on a mathematical
plain of flatness all the way to those mountains, miles away,
that rise abruptly as rough pyramids from a lake of sand.

Since our home acres in Michigan are a forest and our
house is set in wooded hills that roll like lush women, close
and intimate, the distance here is intoxicating and addictive,
and we can't get enough. It is no wonder we don't see what's
coming, and at first are merely distracted by the dark silhouette of a man, off to the side. Or is it two men? They shimmer
in the heat, distorted. Then we see the flashing lights of what
can only be a police cruiser.

David slows. I lean forward in disbelief, already trying to
make this something other than what is.

I am the kind of person who, on the outside, looks like a
team player. And in behavior, most people think I am. I will

contribute, speak appropriately, work hard, make the "right" decision, though if you know me well, you will see how, for me, the right decision might twist. My public persona is made of focused self-control and gentle will, and if you couple these attributes with inherited Catholic guilt and a hard-won aware- ness of cause and effect, you have a decent model of good citizenship. But I have a lawless mind, the kind that veers off and sheers away and doesn't really like being told what is real. It is a bird that won't light but flies obsessively on some un- charted migration. The brain makes wild associations, hearing things other, telling itself interconnected tales, though not so intelligently as to be truly Joycean, but enough so that it never settles easily into reality. When pushed, it becomes outright mutinous, searching for a better story, some mysterious ought- to-be.

So I cannot believe what we have stumbled upon. Other possibilities dart into my head. I imagine the uniformed man is helping the smaller, darker man as they walk up the road; maybe a hubcap popped off, and they are both looking for it. Or the officer is going to take the man to the nearest gas station to help him fill his gas tank. Perhaps the smaller man is leading the cop to a place where they will, together, solve some crime. Maybe they are going to lift up and fly like birds, and it will be a story to tell once we are home, and our friends will ask how we got hold of that dried peyote.

But even as my mind is offering these imaginings, I know it is only because the opposite must be true.

Here is trouble in its moment.

Still it doesn't come to me, the obvious thing. I am from the North, very near the friendly border of Canada, where we cross easily back and forth, exchanging news with the guards, declaring our six pack and two bottles of wine while they wryly survey the camp gear tangled in the back of the car, where they wave us through in minutes with half-amused, half-bored expressions.

Our car gradually overtakes and draws parallel with the pair of men. David slows, for he too is curious, and we draw nearly abreast. They are walking, their backs to us, on the left side of the road, toward the cruiser parked in the distance. At that angle, from the passenger side, I look through the windshield, a little ahead and then as we move, past David's profile, out his window. We are nearly stopped, and the scene unfolds, framed through the window as though in a film. The man with the dark Latino features is walking ahead of the police officer, who is not a police officer exactly, but a border guard strapped with a leather holster and wearing one of those wide-brimmed but too-small hats that are supposed to keep the sun off all the way around. I see, in those brief seconds, that the Latino man is handcuffed and that his slight frame is bent with the kind of despair you see in war marches.

And then, perhaps because we have slowed, perhaps because he feels my voyeuristic interest, he glances up and we make brief, intense eye contact before David pulls the car past. The glance is enough—resistance, defiance, resigned dignity. My brain reels up, startled, recognizing both expression and bone structure, ranging into memory, years back, searching, *what is it* . . . there: In one of my first teaching classrooms in a rural community, among the many migrant and immigrant students who passed through my classes, there was one particular student who claimed my attention differently than the others.

A teenaged boy who had at first claimed he was from Texas had been put into my basic English class. He was impatient with the practice reading, and when I approached him about his attitude, he told me they were "baby stories." When, trying to assess his ability, I asked him what he liked to read, he told me *Don Quixote* and Borges. He said his mother read Marquez to him. I remember looking closely at his face. There it was—defiance, and that quiet if battered dignity. I asked, *Where are you from?* and he named, in a Spanish accent, a location with which I was unfamiliar, and when, merely to confirm my realization, I asked, *Mexico?* he answered a different question with curt pride: *No. Mayan.*

I realized only through research what claiming Mayan ancestry meant in the subcultures of Mexico. That he would eschew as his ancestors the Spanish invaders and claim one of the most accomplished of indigenous peoples as his own signaled a rare understanding both of history and his own genealogy—and an independence and pride I respected.

Though I stopped giving him "baby stories," the boy left without a good-bye in late October when the apple processing was done. But what I remember most was his blazing resistance to being pegged, that look after he had patiently proven that he was utterly literate in his own language and sophisticated enough to follow the narrative structure of Marquez, albeit with his mother's help, and that he claimed his Mayan ancestry as a direct link to a culture of kings.

Though the man being apprehended on an Arizona highway is not the same person, that look of defiance, resistance, and yes, through it all, dignity, is the same. And because I am absorbed in the look, the memory, the look again, I do not see the intersection coming.

A sudden physical alertness in David turns me away from the long stare at the men, now behind us, and back to the blacktop. In front of us, cars line up at a four-cornered crossroads in the middle of the desert, which looks like a huddled village of semis, battered vans, and Porta Potties. There are several patrol cars, and longer, permanent-looking trailers with tinted windows.

"What's going on?"

"I think this is a border check."

"We're miles north of the border."

"This highway comes from the border. They must check here, too." He hesitates, sighs. "Probably looking for illegals coming through the desert."

How stupid of me. Of course there would be checks farther north, farther from the border. Of course, if you made it across the border, there would be other places where you could be caught. I just had no idea.

We stop at the signal. Two border patrol officers approach the car in that slow deliberate walk of people constantly on guard. I imagine for a moment that we have left an empty suitcase in the back, that perhaps it is covered with a picnic blanket and looks like something other than what it is, and that that will be enough: they will haul us out and search us, and we will have a pretty good story to tell when we finally get home.

But there is no suitcase, and my paranoia is misplaced. Nothing dramatic happens. It is enough that guards approach each side of the car, lean down enough that they may peer into our open windows, that they are big, serious men who do not smile. They look at us, not as individuals but as though memorizing our features and comparing them to the features on our driver's licenses. Their holsters are packed with real guns on level with my eyes as they bend to take our rental papers, ask us to *Open the trunk, please.* Finally, they step back, return the licenses. They do not wish us a good day or trip or vacation but wave us through and turn to the next vehicle.

We roll forward in that now-brilliant sunlight, which, without the speed of the car to mimic a breeze, makes the air heavy and acrid. As we slowly accelerate, we pass again the officer and the man from the road, now walking up the roughly carpentered stairs of one of the trailers. The guard unlocks it and points the man inside. And then we pass a van, and the back is open, and in it sit several men in dark work clothes, none of them peering out and none with any expression on his face as clear as the one on the face of the man we have just passed. And I realize with a start that before the end of the day, the van will be full, and the guards will haul these men away, south on this same highway, back across the border over which they have come.

I am silent all the way to the Dragoon Mountains, filled not with defiance but with hopelessness, for I know this is not a simple problem. I am safe, well-fed, employed, a citizen. And another human being who does not have what I have goes to extraordinary and illegal lengths to solve that set of problems. I don't know what to think or say about it.

Then I remember the Apache story: *The One Who Made the Earth told them to move to a new location, and when they did, they slept well, and liked it and lived in a good way.*

Deep in the Dragoons, light straight out of a Thomas Cole painting drenches the crests. David is a shadow at the dark intersection of trails below, waiting for me to make the decision. I stand still watching, waiting, hoping for . . . a cure. The N'de believed that these mountains were alive, the home of supernaturals called "mountain people." They believed the mountains were protectors from illness, the source of power, teachers of the songs and sacred knowledge.

I stand there, remembering the man with defiant eyes stepping into the trailer, followed by the officer with his impassive, guarded face. Were there papers inside, a thousand forms, filing drawers, the sour hymn of computers, more men in uniform with unsmiling faces? The air would feel close after the open desert, maybe chilly from the air conditioners turned on too high. They would stand before each other, and there would be questions without good answers.

The man might look at the forms and sigh, and in the sigh there might be a song, one that could not be ignored, a song with the hot sun in it, a song of cool water and the call of the nightbirds at dusk over land that no longer yields. A song of the man's older sister and her little boy, and his mother reading to the boy.

The officers guarding the man who sighs might feel something in their own breath, in their hands, as if they too would like to sing, words about a cactus in bloom, a son who has begun kindergarten, a mother hooked to a dialysis machine, all that coupled with the drumming of their own hearts as they stand in a silence that is full of words not yet sung.

Who will make the songs heard?

I turn away from David, waiting, and look into the distant ridge, where surely there are caves that could hold a song, a spirit. I search the creek bed, where a being might flit and play in the low thickets. I want to call out, *Are you there?* How long would I have to search the crevasses to find a boy with a proud Mayan face, a would-be immigrant with rebellious eyes, a defiant leader? Cochise, what led you? Did the mountain people speak to you?

There, the high scarred spires, still visible in the almost-gone light. They are aloof, singing in the dying light of dust and red earth and time. Would they heal us? I see them breaking away from their ridge, the shear of boulders falling away to reveal stone-and-flesh beings, and I see them walking to the four corners and opening their mouths and singing a healing vision into the future.

Here is the guard, taking off the handcuffs.

Here is the border-crosser working in a classroom.

Here is a boy grown up, reading Marquez to his daughter.

Here is Cochise, riding a horse out of the shadows into some whole and transformed final days in the mountains he loved and where he left his body.

Would he tell me the story of hope and transformation instead of bitter revenge?

David calls softly, "Are you there?" And in his voice, my reality. I am not naïve. This is the desert night coming on. Cochise is dead, his body hidden, gone to dust somewhere in these mountains. I will not find it. I turn back, climbing slowly down into the shadows, taking the impact of the rocky terrain with my aching legs and scraped feet. I make my way to David, who hands me water, and I drink. We look at each other; we know each other. He has wisely called me back from many brinks, this not the last. It is almost night in the gulch, though the mountain peaks are topped by eerie golden light streaking across the sky above us. Now we can see the path but little else. High on the ridge, the silhouette of a coyote shivers into shadow. Small creatures scuttle in the gravel, scratching toward the pungent darkness.

In this near dark, turning away from the heights, I know my lawless mind had wanted to find not the literal Cochise, but the Cochise of my childhood, the outlaw hero who might live eternally in these mountains, who in my fantasy was never tainted by the powers that categorized him as less than human but was always more like the young student who read Marquez or Borges, who would not be categorized as stupid,

or like the man who, even in handcuffs, could make eye contact and whose subverted dignity defied that he was a criminal.
Instead, I must try to see in the dark, to find my way along a
rough path, going backwards.

Driving back to Bisbee, we come again to those four corners. It is full dark at the crossroads, but spotlights blaze like
tall sentries, casting down wide funnels of light that encom-
pass the buildings. The van is gone, but the border guards are
still there, carrying out this hard ceremony. Again we slow,
again they flag us, again the serious review of our licenses,
papers, trunk. We are waved forward. We drive south through
the desert.

I think of the man who looked back at me. Where is he
now? Is he home? Is he in some sad camp on the other side? Is
he already hiding in the shadows by that long river ironically
called the Rio Grande, waiting for another chance to swim
over? Is he plotting with a coyote, a man who might help him
or might take his money and leave him to die? Perhaps he is
headed even now for mountains where he believes he will be
safe, or where he may die and his body will never be found.

But then, as we drive the highway south, I remember the
story: From the mountains, the mountain people learned the
curing ceremonies. *Then The One Who Made the Earth said,*
"Why don't you go to the sick men and say some words over them
and make them well." Make them well. For the renegade Cochise, for the man in handcuffs, for the boy who read Marquez,
for lawmakers and border guards, I want a curing ceremony.
As we drive through a dark, star-studded desert night, I know
why it is so hard to leave these mountains: Cochise is not here,
but there are people who have his defiance, his vision, his will
to survive—they are here. They can be found. In response to
their shared resistance, a lawless mind might take flight, might

dare to hope for something better. For the boy, the border-crosser, the lost integrity of Cochise, the lawless dreams of my own lost childhood, I want the mountain people, someone, to say the words over all of us so we can be *made well*.

The Underpass

Washington DC

In that long-past January, the month we inaugurate presidents, I had forgotten my socks. It was 1973. I stood, chilled and tired, in the proverbial shadow of the Washington Monument with my boyfriend, Vern, and a crowd of other long-haired, bearded, and bedraggled protesters, mostly college students but also gray-haired grandmas and older men in tattered pea coats. That was the year we had participated in too many protests to remember, had canvassed hard for McGovern and lost, and eighteen hours previous had climbed into an unheated van in the middle of the night to drive from Grand Valley State College in Michigan to Washington DC to protest a corrupt man and a corrupt war and who knows what other corruptions. The list was out there, and though I don't discount its sincerity, I could no longer give concrete rationale about why I was there.

I had forgotten socks and my feet were numb.

On the platform, a black woman railed against this re-elected president, and by some strange catch in the wind, we could also hear tinny fragments, muted phrases, a stately word here and there, of the second inauguration of President Nixon. Through some sound system that must have been enormous and pervasive but ineffective, these halfwords, carried to us in a metallic flutter, mixed with the rally's protest language to spill a linguistic American pie of distortion into the cold air.

I remember the words of neither speech because suddenly, whether due to cold feet or a cold heart, none of it made sense anymore.

At that time, I made an impulsive vow never to return to that city, that particular protest also marking the end of my overt political activism. Like many of us from that time, I hit an invisible emotional wall and became apolitical. In the decades since, I have turned to quieter efforts, focused on local projects, particularly around food and sustainable agriculture. I learned to cherish my friends and community, and when possible, to change small elements of the ordinary. I learned to write and have taught young writers as best I could, with an acute awareness of my limitations.

That day in 1973 marked the end of both a literal and figurative journey. The previous night I had helped navigate a van into Washington, had listened to talk of revolution in a basement house in Maryland and opted for the peaceful march instead of throwing rocks at the cops on a certain corner, had come out into the light of a cold, damp day, one of some ten thousand people who gathered at the Lincoln Memorial and

marched to the Washington Monument—events of some
three decades ago. Who would have thought I'd even be alive
now? But I am, and in my quiet teacherly life, one of my dear-
est students has won a national prize. I am invited to watch
Beth receive the award and to be recognized as her teacher at
the Kennedy Center.

Susceptible as I am to honors, I decide to return to the city
I have shunned.

The ceremony is scheduled for 1:00, and if David and I
want to see some sights, we won't have time to return to the
hotel. We dress for the day. I slip on a long tunic-style dress
with wildflowers, dressy but midwestern. I slip into heels and
pretty up the way David likes. We'll go early to some monuments, see what it feels like, maybe retrace my protester's
march. *Wouldn't that be a hoot?* And while we are that close, we
will take in the Vietnam Memorial. That casual.

I won't be able to remember their names.

When we climb out of the cab, I am distracted, thinking
about Beth and meeting her family later in the day, about the
ceremony and where the other teachers are from and if I remembered to bring business cards, materials about the school,
an extra notebook. We climb out of the cab and start down the
walkway toward the wall. I am chattering and simultaneously
rummaging in my purse for a notebook to add something to
my list of things not to forget. I am snapping my purse when I
look up, stumble, catch myself, slow down, am undone. I step
toward the wall, silent now, all ordinary thought erased. Here
are their names. All along that slick and momentous length are
names that, from a step back become human texture in stone,
a dark and implacably shining mirror that represents a border
we have not crossed but once crossed is crossed forever.

I thought the names would come back, those two boys I

knew from college, who went over and did not come back. I
remember their faces, so I thought the names would come up,
trip off the tip of my tongue, and I would be able to just walk
over and touch the names and say a prayer. But when I come
closer and see, for the first time, that impenetrable marble written over with the hieroglyphs of loss, I can't remember them.
Then, in that awful anonymity, all the names, every one of
them stand out to me, become small stars. I come close, touch
the dark surface, pull away, step close again, run my fingers
down a row—was it you? Or you? I knew their names when
I had been protesting a President's Watergate, and during the
final throes of Vietnam. I knew their names when I graduated
from college and went for my master's. I knew their names to
tell students sadly in my first years of teaching, and later when
students would ask about "the sixties," which weren't quite the
sixties for me. I knew their names when I went to reunions,
weddings, baptisms, even funerals. Not anymore.

But here are all the names, and now those two could be any
of these. David's arm slips around me as we walk the walk,
scanning them, me telling him I will *pull them up* from my unconscious, yet unable to muster even a letter, though other
things return cinematically clear: The boy I liked a lot from my
Shakespeare class at college left at semester to enlist. He once
complimented me on my reading of pentameter, and I must
have flirted, because I remember his smiles; he sat next to me
from *The Comedy of Errors* to *Hamlet*. We never dated, did we?
I think we both had steadies. I am ashamed to say now, I probably despised the fact that he enlisted, but I don't remember
my reaction one way or the other. The other boy, a skinny red-
head, came to mass and church activities and sang those Good
News folk songs with such a boyish robustness that I teased
him. He was drafted—I think there may have been credit is-

sues or maybe he wasn't in school at all but just came to campus mass to be near us—he seemed a little needy—and though he had been encouraged to go to Canada, he decided to take his chances.

So much is gone. I don't remember saying good-bye to either of them. But I remember the news when it came, sometime in the next year for both of them. In '70 or '71? I remember spring, the campus rolling with green, corn just planted in the distant fields. How could I forget their names? My youth is staring back at me from the shiny wall mottled with names.

We stay there too long, me pacing the length of the wall twice, touching the small script here and there, letting the now hallowed names come in through my fingertips, unable to leave. David is as quiet and touched as I am, though steady in his fine way.

Finally we turn away, and David stops and makes me drink some water. After a while we decide to walk, to take a path around and over to the Lincoln Memorial, though I cannot, for all the deep breathing and brisk steps, get my face dry. Is that why, when I arrive to look up at the famous Lincoln face, I am filled with awe and old loss renewed? Those young men were already dead when I came here on that January day in '73, already dead when I stood near the shrubbery at the side, stamping my feet to create some kind of heat in them, waiting for the motion of the crowd to begin its slow gesture toward the monument. I remember wrapping my arms around myself, trying to keep a brisk wind out of my light jacket, and being hungry and having no money and being angry at myself for forgetting to put on socks in the middle of the night when we had left Michigan to drive to Washington DC.

Then we started to sing, and the crowd leaders moved out onto the street, carrying placards, setting the pace, which I remember as funereal. The first marchers moved long before the last marchers, but gradually, from stragglers to militants, we all joined, and the wind off the Potomac turned colder. There was a mist when we finally walked the slow walk, singing the songs we all knew, down the long street to the Washington Monument. All this comes back to me as I stare up at the carved face of the man who, nearly a century and a half before, against all odds, warred the country back together.

When I stood under this face as that long-ago girl, I mocked statuary in general, and those built to past leaders particularly. That attitude, too, has softened. Now I see Lincoln's stone face as a complicated representation. Calm inevitability, a strange weariness. The history that has grown in me since I was twenty is the lens through which I see it now. As I stare up at him, my breathing rights, and I take in his sadness for the first time.

David is close, reminds me of the time. We walk out from the shadow, and I vow to focus on the wonder of this clear day, the green lawn, the cool June air, a dear student.

I don't remember why we decided to walk to the Kennedy Center. I don't know why we didn't go back to the Wall and catch a cab. Perhaps I didn't want to go back, so angry and sad at what I had forgotten—and remembered. Maybe we walked because in the far distance we could see the flat top of the Kennedy Center, and so, in the clear air, it seemed close.

We have no map, haven't bargained for the circling walks, the streets that seem to head in one direction and then curve in another. We haven't bargained for the slow realization that, in this most groomed of American cities, we have to hike across a wide expanse of only partly civilized field. As we cross it, the Kennedy disappears behind a bank of highway, and we figure out that we will need to follow a berm and then a shallow trough, cross under an abandoned overpass and then actually climb the bank of the overpass to the highway, and finally cross the highway to the Center. We realize how complicated this will be, and how strange, here in the nation's capital, much too late to turn back and find a cab, too late to change course, because now we don't know how to get there any other way and still be on time. *So like the way I've run my life,* I mutter to David as we are tromping through stickers and bristly grass, the memorials now out of sight behind the berm and traffic.

From a distance it all looks possible, and we are country people who walk a lot. But the grass is littered with broken bottles, and shards and bags of plastic catch in the untrimmed shrubbery, twisting in the twigs. We keep tromping, me lifting the skirt under my tunic. I am trying not to notice the wicked blister forming on my heel, trying not to think about the distant highways with a clear view of this field, of people in cars and cabs and buses who are looking at us from their air-conditioned vehicles and asking themselves *what the hell* we are doing out here. We must look like something from a bad indie movie, David in a tie, me in heels, crossing the medians, heading for a highway that won't have a stoplight for miles. As we near the underpass, I see how we will have to walk under it in order to climb the weed-laden bank on the other side. I fall a little behind in my heels. I don't understand when David stops and waits for me. And then, as I come close, I see what he sees.

To get to the highway, we must pass through someone's home.

Listen, people live here. It is their home we trespass on. How have we come so close? How, in the middle of Washington DC, have we stumbled off the tidy sidewalks assigned to proper pedestrians?

Because it is not a home the way a home should be. It is rough shelter tucked against the cement pilings because the overpass keeps off the rain, protects from the sun, at least until late in the day. And the ditch—yes we now know it is a dry ditch, not a path, we are following—leads directly under this overpass spackled with plastic bags and Coke bottles and soggy paper like dirty snow. David motions me to come, and I stare at him and look back to see if yet again, I've missed some quiet cul-de-sac where a cab will be waiting to whisk us away. Then I turn to him and take the steps in silence.

There are two who live there, and they have made a place to sleep of a refrigerator box and some tarp, maybe part of a tent. We follow the path next to them, and though I try not to meet their eyes, the younger man utters a sound with a question in it, and I glance at him, too used to responding to voice. The other, rail thin, leaning on his elbow in a ragged sleeping bag, shakes his head at our ignorance and stupidity. He smokes a cigarette, and after we have passed, swears. Everywhere, the plastic bags rustle, though I can feel no breeze. The scent fills my lungs.

And what am I doing again in this city that breaks my heart on so many levels? For, no doubt, here is yet another forgotten pair of names. We build monuments to the great leaders so that we won't forget their names, their virtues of wisdom, bravery, or dedication, and we build memorials to those who have lost their lives, so we won't forget their names or their sacrifice. Despite the grandeur of these gestures, the personal connection to history is what makes meaning, or so I think. And then the plastic snaps, the grasses rustle. The man behind me swears again. But I, I have forgotten.

Forgive us our trespasses . . .

We climb the bank, me struggling in my heels. The noise of traffic rises like thunder. I lose a shoe and stand in my hose in the grass. Struggling with the strap inside the reverberation of hundreds of cars, I feel the blister break. What is it with my feet and this city? By the time we scale the bank, rising ridiculously at the guardrail on the side of a highway streaming with speeding traffic, I am drenched with sweat. Memories like small angry birds dive out of the air—cold feet, a boy's red hair, the muddle of the loudspeaker—and join the buzz of frustration as I face the highway. My gut tightens as I stare across the street at the stately Center, its white columns gleaming in the sharp sunlight. David looks for a way to cross, a place marked for pedestrians, but there are only speed signs, the lots on the other side marked with letters of the alphabet A, B, C. Even the signs, *DO NOT ENTER, EXIT HERE, SPEED BUMP AHEAD,* and all the arrows pointing away do not offer a clue as to how to cross.

In the midst of the growl of traffic, I think about the men under the bridge. I think of the Wall and of Lincoln, of the march thirty years ago where, after the long file to the mall in the drizzle, the huddling in the cold, the distorted speeches, I finally left the protesters and walked the city streets. I looked at the houses of Washington DC, at the tidy and gracious lawns, at the iron gates, and the ornate doors. I remember passing an embassy. I remember being awed that people lived in homes that had such history, and still so little seemed to change, so much seemed corrupt. When I returned to the protest to sing the final songs, I had decided I would never come again.

Now, I look at the majestic building across the street, a place where a good thing will happen, a young woman will receive recognition for writing brave poems and plays, and I will be there to witness, which, after all these years, is what I have done best. I look at the signs, reading something more in them than what they mean. In a lull, I can still hear the plastic bags snapping their gray words.

George? Bill?

And what about the names of the men below us?

And in that moment, ironically, the very loss of that connection makes meaning. The Lincoln Memorial means more because I have forgotten the bitterness of that damp march and its chilly disillusion, and in yet another twist of memory, the Wall means more because I have forgotten the names of my lost friends and now assume any name might be one of theirs. Memory is an unpredictable witness, but in reclaiming even the emptiness, we shape our narratives for . . . what? A new action, a different march?

So what of the living?

What of these forgotten men who claim a shabby privacy in the middle of the most public city in our nation? If I were given their names, would I write them on a wall? Or would I forget their names and try to feed them?

What have I done in these thirty years?

I lift my skirts and straddle the guardrail and step forward as dozens of cars hit their brakes and horns.

Where Angels Are

Great Smoky Mountains National Park,
Tennessee and North Carolina

I. LOOKING

"What are angels made of?" I ask my mother.

"The same stuff as we are, but better."

"In the pictures they look like smoke."

"That's what I mean."

I will ask her again.

On the eve of the second war in Iraq, David and I take a vacation. It is not a thing we would have planned; the two things simply happen simultaneously, in March of 2003, the onset of the war and our spring break from Interlochen Arts Academy in Michigan. With a kind of helpless awe, we have watched the shift in weathers: on military bases throughout the country, the grueling ritual of preparation, and in Michigan, a winter storm so bad it brings down two of our most mature wild cherry trees. In our northern life, we have driven icy roads to work, listening to the news, too many mornings; we have caught each other staring over the snowy landscape with a blankness that can hurt you if you stay too long in it. The world is a juxtaposition of media images and late winter, both exhausting.

Not knowing just when this invasion-that-is-not-an-invasion will happen, we plan the precious weeks of spring break to travel south to one of our nation's oldest and most popular destinations, the Great Smoky Mountains National Park. It is a park balanced on the border between two states, Tennessee and North Carolina, and perhaps between two states of mind as well. Despite its dedication to wilderness, it is one of the most visited—some would say over-visited—parks in the nation. Still, this great eastern divide holds the romance of the Appalachian Trail, the freshness of spring rivers, the opportunity to look again at each other.

To turn off the news.

But as our small Jeep covers the highway miles from Northern Michigan to these southern states, David cannot resist; hourly he flips on the news, tracking the releases. Even though his calm face grows more serious with every report of this old progress called war, he would rather know than not know. We learn that just this morning Al Qaeda forces have called for Jihad as U.S. forces gather near the borders.

The highway hums in quiet violence under our tires.

That evening, tucked in a mountainside cabin on the Tennessee side, we sit in the small, rustic living room, listening to the reports. I cannot watch the screen but look away to the table, the couch, the arm of the recliner, where my eyes linger over the woven patterns of a sixties-style afghan of bright orange and brown, and I run my fingers in and out of the soft old weave. I am holding it as comfort against the language that fills my ears from the small TV.

On my orders . . .

These are the opening stages . . .

I want Americans to know . . .

David tells me the third infantry division is going into Iraq now. He reminds me this is the standing infantry division both our fathers fought in during World War II. It has been in existence since World War I. It has one of the most distinguished histories in the military, but over the wars and years, over fifty thousand men have been lost from it. In that division, David's father was wounded in the hand and arm and eventually discharged—his hand never again the same. My father was scarred as well, but differently. I walk out of the Tennessee cabin, trying to see nothing but this rugged tree-covered mountainside, to feel nothing but the soft crocheted blanket in my hands and smell the gentility, the integrity of this small, square, human-made thing, to hold it against the unmaking that will take place across the warp of the planet.

The war has begun.

II. THE APPALACHIAN TRAIL

"They are eternal," she tells me. "In that they are not like us.
    They stay with you always."

"Are they by us right now?"

"You don't know when they are near," she says. "But they walk
    the same paths we do."

The Appalachian Trail, built in 1932 and now one of the most famous hiking paths in our country, spans the country in an irregular diagonal from Georgia to Maine and is considered by serious hikers to be a lifetime achievement. Deep in the Great Smoky Mountains National Park, the trail follows roughly the state lines along the high point of a major mountain ridge for seventy-plus miles. After a few days of preliminary hikes in this region full of challenging hikes, we gain some courage and decide to try one popular section of the Appalachian Trail, a mere four miles from Newfound Gap to Charlie's Bunion, a precipice named for its shape. We have been told we can hike there by lunch if we start early, and I think to myself, it's only four miles; we'll be there in plenty of time. But as soon as we are beyond the mile marker—a north-viewing lookout where most people turn back—we are once again caught in the refrain from the hiking book, "Up and down the trail goes." Up and down we go through ravaged forest, which opens to views of Mount LeConte and the Oconaluftee River watershed.

What I didn't expect was the water. Water, water, everywhere. It's spring in the mountains, after all, and here, it's not cold enough to make snow, thank goodness, but it's not fully warm yet either, and it's been raining. My shoes, light hikers, are soaked within the first hour and stay that way. Despite the beauty of an early spring canopy of young wild cherry, yellow birch, beech and an undergrowth thick with blackberry, I am preoccupied by my slogging through an ankle-deep creek that is really the gullied-out trail, pocked and clotted with stones. I make a lot of noise clomping over the stones, trying to keep my balance, telling myself that this creek-as-trail should be no surprise. Here in these old mountains, the creeks were trail makers, funneling a way down the mountain, shaping a path over stones. Still, silly of me not to have sealed the old shoes.

My feet will be cold the entire hike.

I think of the words of last night's speech: *"a campaign on the harsh terrain . . . could be more difficult . . . than some predict."*

I think of desert—sand, dust.

We have chosen a "tame" section of the trail. None of the summits are much higher than six thousand feet, and much of the forest is decimated by the balsam woolly adelgid; thus the woods are thinner and more open than they once were. Still, I begin to understand the trail's reputation. The trail carries the dangers of wilderness and other elements. The lore covers bear attacks, spider bites, snake visitations, threats of wild hogs, off-season snow storms, and travelers who stumbled, became lost, or were robbed or raped—for the trail has attracted a cross section of human beings—all of it warns us to pay attention. But if none of those threats play out, here is the ordinary threat.

How is a mountain like a sponge?

It holds water.

Ever flowing, it springs from clefts and feeds the gravity-tugged creeks flowing down these mountains to the reservoirs. Even on the high, flat-topped ridges, small pools spread their muddy silk directly across the path, rising from rivulet springs, held right at the brink of the ridge where North Carolina falls away to the south and Tennessee to the north. We did not comprehend this simpler treachery, that while the vistas would open and there would be the Shaconage—*place of blue smoke,* the Cherokee called it—the trail itself would demand such attention. We are alone in the creek-funneled ravines, in places where it would be difficult to find rescue if we slipped or fell or even got so cold we became hypothermic. Step carefully. This is the Appalachian. Walk with . . . what is it? Attention.

But I am in the place of blue smoke.

The news. The news.

Lori Piestewa is the first woman soldier to die. She is lost. Or rather, her convoy takes a wrong turn in the desert. Blue smoke.

The last rise to Charlie's Bunion, an outcropping of gray slate shaped roughly like a giant's toe thrust upward to the winds as though to air it out, is spiraled by a lesser path that breaks from the main trail. Legend tells that this precipice is named after a local mountaineer, one Charlie Conner, by his friends during a visit in 1929. He apparently had some kind of foot trouble, his friends had a sense of humor, and thus, the formation was named. We scramble up this rougher terrain, straddling the angular sections of broken rock, giggling with relief, and set ourselves into a rock bluff overlooking a drop of several hundred feet. Big view. We look at each other for the first time in a mile, tension draining from our faces. David leans back against jagged slabs, stretching muscles strung tight as wire. I share commonplaces with a dad day-hiking with his kids. His children, goatlike and quick, seem barely affected by the intensity of the trail. They scuffle loose stones over the edge, flirting with the drop, and listen for the stones to strike the rocks below. Whether lost in wind or foliage, the sound of the rocks hitting the lower surface never returns to us, though the twelve-year-old claims he hears it *miles down.*

We wiggle into fresh socks, knowing our feet will be wet again, but for now there will be the reprieve of dryness. From our daypacks, we eat sandwiches, apples, chips. I stare at the distant peaks that mark the main range of the Appalachian. They have names like poems—Laurel Top and Sequoyah—but they are founded in the Anakeesta Formation—shattered slate. This precipice, named after a toe, is brittler and more dan-

gerous than the more distant Smokies, which are formed of
Thunderhead sandstone, dense and smoother. Thus the ominous name for this jagged range: The Sawteeth. Because this
rock is so heavily splintered, hikers sometimes fall. We move
back from the edge, lie down on the rock in the cool sun, close
our eyes. I think we doze.

Lori Piestewa is a Hopi from Arizona.

I imagine the shards of rock dropping miles down, dropping
for so long that they lose their stone nature and grow wings,
feathered appendages, an anomaly in the style of Magrittes's
airborne locomotive. I see the stones flying, their inner still-
ness caught in the rush of air, their hearts that beat once every
thousand years starting with awareness: *What is this, what is
this?*

How does a convoy get lost? The convoy was on the wrong
road, ended up in a town called Nasiriya, where according to
their maps, no town should have been. How did that happen?

*. . . praying that all those who serve will return safely and soon
. . .*

We run out of water.

It is glib to say mistakes are made.

What were we thinking? The irony of worrying about water while standing in the shallows of a mountain-creek trail
makes both of us smile wryly. But we have been clearly warned
not to drink from the creeks. I tip my water bottle to my lips;
it really is empty. I am thirsty, and I know I must already be a
little dehydrated.

They say in the deserts of Iraq, dehydration is a huge problem for soldiers.

We aim for Icewater Spring, a day shelter where we can
refill.

What drives a person to be among the hundred plus each year who *do* the Appalachian Trail, enduring the threat of everything from water-borne bacteria to bear attack, to make every day the calculation that is skill against accident, intelligence against will or foolishness? What does it mean to walk these American miles, trek with a kind of soldierly strength over the rough terrain, to see the country from the inside out? Certainly it is an honor to accomplish this, and pride must, to some degree, drive the hiker.

Does the same apply to soldiers?

One of the first victims of this war is a young marine, a Guatemalan with permanent U.S. status named José Gutierrez, a man who joined the forces so he could send money home to his sister.

People take care of their families in whatever way they can.

Convoys have maps, don't they?

Skilled, smart hikers pay attention to their water supply.

I am thirsty, but I know it is only a small discomfort.

What happens in a desert?

The far-flung day shelters of the Appalachian Trail are of similar architecture, a structural mix of openness to the world and protection from the elements. Most are built of stone and log, lean-to style with shed roofs, open on the high front, partly enclosed on the sides, fully enclosed at the back. In front, a rugged yard for sitting and gathering, but inside, a space shadowy and cavelike. Rough boards floor two levels, the hearth level and then a step up to a higher level, where these strangers unroll sleeping bags to lie down side by side for the night. Here, even sleep is communal.

This shelter can house a crowded sixteen.

Midafternoon, and the deeply coombed fireplace is still

cold, though a stone bench is already draped with sweatpants and gear clothes. This is the point in the day when the hikers who have committed to the weeks or months to hike the trail find the shelters and eat and rest from the grind of this relentless up and down. They would have planned how much time it would take to arrive at a shelter, claim a space, prepare a meal, clean up, store the food, and carry out basic toiletries before bedding down next to strangers.

They would collect and filter water.

I sit on the step at the entrance, not fully entering, because I am trying to be respectful of those who must make real preparations. I am a day hiker; I will hike back to some place where a hot shower and a soft mattress are a few steps from each other. Now that we have water, I am as safe as one can be in a National Park in the middle of America.

How does it feel to be unsafe all the time?

At the threshold, I watch a tall woman unpack inside the shelter. As I watch her, I realize she is doing it. She is one of those doing the AT, the entire trail. She is dressed in gray insulated underwear, baggy with wear, marked with a circle of bottom grime from sitting so often on the ground. She wears a waffle-weave T-shirt with long sleeves, the cuffs so ragged they hang in strands, and an insulated vest the color of dirty silver that absorbs and distributes heat. She hangs her gear over beams to air out and sets up a small single-flame stove for cooking. Slim and muscular, her body moves with an unconscious aloofness molded by knowing exactly how much energy she has in reserve and how she must use it. In her face: a tired friendliness and resigned caution. She smiles but does not speak. She tears opens a foil packet and begins to pour dehydrated rice into the small pot of hot water.

I want to speak to her, step into what is now clearly her kitchen territory. I want to hear her story, decipher her face. There is something clear and precise, some pure thing in her sunburned, freckled skin. I clear my throat. She glances over but does not slow. She is about her business on her trail, her work.

David brings me the shelter's journal, where one hiker has written simply, "Fog sucks," and another, passing through just the day before, has written a long entry about his concerns regarding the war, about what the Iraqi people there will suffer in the face of such destruction. After David closes the book, I gratefully sip the water he has brought, stare out at the terrain veiled in blue smoke.

Behind me, the woman steps from wall to bench and back.

What are the coming hours like for her? For each of the hikers? After each has claimed space to sleep, will they share food? I like to think she would, that certain ones, traveling in close proximity to each other and settling in the same shelters at night, might become friendly, might pool resources.

Before dark, two or three will gather all the food and, several hundred feet away, hang it from lines high over an arching branch strung with a series of pulleys and lines. In the final light, each surveys the yard to make sure every scrap of litter and every T-shirt is gathered up and taken in, anything that might attract bears.

I imagine the skinniest, wiriest one would build and feed the night fire.

I imagine this woman would be the one to make sure every hiker is under the shelter, to check that the last hiker is back from the loo, a distant composting toilet almost filled to the brim. Then the most important act of the night's preparations: unrolling a chain link fence that is coiled in a roll and tied to the eaves. The campers, under stuttered flashlight or dim moon, untie the heavy woven fencing, let drop this steel cross-hatching over the three open sides so that the bears cannot come in and take them. In the end, the woman and the others will sleep in this outdoor cage where they are safe, depending on the temperament of those who are in the cage with them. Trust and caution sleep side by side. Something about . . . *our common defense* . . .

Is this how it is for soldiers?

David massages my knee, and we rise to take on the final miles back to the Gap. Before I leave, I turn to her—this woman of the trail. Her feet and mine have crossed the same stones, if only briefly. She pauses, meets my gaze, nods and gives me a look of such integrity that I feel honored for the small acknowledgment. Perhaps she felt my respect, my rough imaginings, my restraint in the face of her work. She had the spirit of one a long time at what she was doing, who knew how to do it, how to take care of herself, how to stay separate from the world but be of it too. All the way back, through the soreness and the progressively slower trekking, I let the independence in her face soften the language that still runs a harrowing noise behind everything I am seeing in these mountains.

We will defend our freedom . . .

Is that what Lori Piestewa was doing? José Gutierrez?

Or were they trying to do something hard and survive with integrity?

III. THE GRANNY HOLE

"They protect us, right?"

"Not always."

"What do they do then?"

"They help you see the hard things."

My mother teaches angels differently from the catechism.

It takes us a while to recover from the Appalachian. Though it was merely a small slice of the real thing, we are tired, and our bodies are aching. And because the news is not good, we find it impossible not to "check in" as David calls his periodic flipping of channels, turning of radio dials. The next day we decide on an easy hike, a walk really, to a place that will give us a taste of the history of the region. In Cades Cove, a historic settlement deep in the west end of the park, we manage a gentle mile to a homestead inhabited by John Oliver and his son Elijah from the 1820s to the time the park was formed in the 1920s. The structures huddle on slopes upland of the coveted bottomland that was level and wet and often rich. The Oliver cabins and barns were remote in a time when remote was the norm, built on transition land between mountain country that the Cherokee inhabited and the villages like Townsend that had sprung up around the lumber industry.

Elijah Oliver's cabin is mud chinked, ax hewn, a hard-core pioneer structure. I enter cautiously, letting my eyes adjust to the dark. No windows. The ceiling is so low that at five and half feet, I duck instinctively—the cross beams that support the loft are that close. The cabin has two fireplaces, but now they hold only March's morning chill, swept clean as the room itself, which is empty and gloomy, though it is a bright day. Too much darkness, I think. Of course, they worked outside much of the day, but still, didn't they want more light? I circle the perimeter of the room carefully as a blind cat, touching the logs, the rough surfaces, feeling my way back to these settlers.

Why is it so dark in here? Did they eschew windows to prevent loss of heat? In a snowy, pervasive mountain winter, that would make sense.

Though I admire their self-sufficiency and simplicity, the bleakness would have hurt my spirit; it seems so large in this small room. Who were the women who tended these fires, who tried to spin or darn socks in this terrible light? And what of the men who came in from the hard work of butchering pigs and planting fields?

What of the work of soldiers? My father peeled potatoes as part of his soldierly duties.

I notice one tiny opening, no more than a narrow slot, low on the wall near the main fireplace. It is barely visible except as a gray spill in the dank air. This would serve as the single window through which the person tending the fire could see the yard and forest. The firekeeper could be sitting in a chair or tending the fire, could lean forward to stir the pot, glance out the hole in the wall and see the light, see who was coming up the back trail. Just this small breath, this moment of reprieve. Such a narrow light. Would the shawled woman sitting in front of the fire, watching a stranger stride up the trail, have risen, added a log, put on water, and turned toward the spare room?

Called the "stranger room," this rough space partitioned from the porch is big enough for only a small bed and a pair of boots. Separate from the communal room, it would have been warm only in summer and an oddity in a house where privacy was rare, where rooms, out of necessity, were held in common. Was it because the Olivers didn't trust visitors, or was it an honor to be given this quietude in the midst of the living in the main room? I turn back to the main room.

Oh, why no windows? And the chill. My fleece can't keep the cold from entering my bones as surely as it must have en-

tered the bones of Elijah's family. I bend again to the firetend-
er's slot. There is the outside, bright with an unspoken spring.
The warmer air spills in, but not much. I run my fingers along
the log butts of the opening, remembering a tour note calls it
a "granny hole." Would the grandmothers sit here and watch
this narrow slice of world? Would the granny have seen the
stranger hurrying up the windy trail? If not light, would she
offer warmth? Would she make a welcome? Was there some
peace after the journey from wherever in the Cove or beyond
the stranger had walked?

Oh, let there have been peace.

David's tall frame blocks the bright doorway, and his steps
are firm on the split plank floor. He has been looking at the architecture of the corncrib, the pig-butchering site. I am squat-
ting in front of the granny hole, babbling my grandmother
fantasy, "I think she sat here. Maybe she couldn't do as much
work, so she watched and welcomed."

David sighs, touches my shoulder. "The granny hole is the
right height to kneel, aim a rifle, and shoot something without
being seen."

"What?"

"There were feuds . . . you know, we read about it."

Oh. That.

In these hills, in these simpler places, wars of community.

Darkness is also a fortress.

We will accept no outcome but . . .

IV. THE LIGHT

> "I don't think they fly; we only wish they would; it's more like
> they fall into the light, and you must have different eyes
> to see them."

"I want to see them."

"Be careful what you wish for."

Our last hike is through river country to Mingo Falls, a falls the Cherokee kept secret, a place where the *river sings*. The path is another rocky thread, but this one stitches the river to the bank, over and back from one side to the other, reflecting my imaginings of the week.

At each of several bridges, fly-fishers cast silver lines through the air, that quick filament of grace extending over the rough foil of fast-moving run-off. Here is higher territory, the voice of water washing out the pain of distorted language. Here is the last bridge, the one that goes nowhere but simply spans the river below Mingo so that one can stand directly below the falls and look up and up into water falling over rock, feel its cold blessing, understand its breaking energies and the nature of falling.

It is the last time I cry.

I would like to say it has the look of wings, this falls, the look of a million feathers tipped to catch the force of motion, not destroyed but blazed open into beauty by the rocks it falls over. And for a moment, the mountain light, often so clipped by height and peak, does open, and something like sun hits the flow and I think it could be so, river falls turned to light and feathers lifting into. . .

Oh, let there be angels.

Let there be people doing their work.

Let us walk the same paths.

Let us greet each other warmly and offer water.

Let us hold each other in our arms, not at arms' length.

Let there be angels.

But I have listened to the contradictions in this walking.

I am also the stranger coming up the path. And there is the granny hole, where perhaps an old one waits to make welcome, or where someone kneels for another purpose. If angels are here, then this park, this American place, this American concept—land held in peace for the pleasure of its people— this natural beauty and light, is now forever linked to the more terrible angel rushing forward in a cascade of the thing we call war.

The blue mountains are constantly walking. If you doubt mountains walking, you do not know your own walking.   *Dōgen, quoting the Chan master Furong*

The Blue Bead

El Yunque, Puerto Rico

I. LATE WINTER

Where is that light we once heard tell of?

In early March, the hills of Leelanau County feel like dark closets, full of some bearish fear. Where my small home perches on the edge of a ravine, the woods and slopes are empty but for the crust of old snow, still two feet deep. Even the deer have moved to the swamps. Inside, my woodstove makes a disturbing ticking, like a clock keeping poor time. The chimney rattles with falling creosote, and the firebox is full, every day, of ash that must be emptied.

In our coastal village of Empire, the temperature drops below ten degrees for ten-plus days. I remind myself how I love falling snow, the immense uncountability of it. And after hard snow, that clean, white horizontal, coupled with the rounding off of summer chairs, all set against the black vertical of tree trunks—the X and Y axes of winter intersected by the flight of red cardinals, the collapsed spheres of small berries, the crooked-coned cedars, the high contrast of dark against white.   But these are ditch days. Gray snow thickens and hardens like diseased skin. And though winter's back will be broken by the equinox, the season dies hard and will kick arctic air at us for another month. Even my beloved David, partner in these seasons, goes quiet. We traipse clumsily among the particulars of bills, groceries, and got-tos. He installs a long-delayed light in a dark closet. It doesn't help.

Where to go to get back whatever it was we had when it wasn't winter?

II. WITHOUT A PASSPORT

We pick her up in the foothills of El Yunque. She has what most people call character but which is really about working in the sun for decades. She has a strong mouth, a lot of lines. Bark-colored eyes that are guarded but not unfriendly. Her face tells me she is who she appears to be.

After today, we will never meet her again.

It's out of character for David and me to pick up hitchhikers, but 191, the narrow jungle highway into El Yunque, is a dead end, several kilometers winding steeply up toward three mountain peaks, where it finally stops at a landslide that has never been repaired. What will it cost her in energy to walk those miles?

When she raises her index finger, I make David stop. I push aside the maps littering the back seat. She climbs in, her quiet "gracias" testing the language barrier, and when I say, "You're welcome," falling by imitation into a voice as soft as hers, she slips into graceful English marked by a Puerto Rican accent.

We choose Puerto Rico because it is as far south as we can go without a passport. Puerto Rico is located at eighteen degrees latitude. A difference of twenty-seven degrees. Set that against single-digit temperatures for ten days straight.

Go as far south as you can and still be in the country.

In the first guidebook we pick up, we discover that in the center of this American commonwealth whose island shore is riddled with tourist traps and high-rise resorts, there exists a mountainous rain forest, El Yunque, the only tropical rain forest in the United States, preserved in a 28,000-acre national park and bordered by undeveloped mountain regions. We have never hiked a rain forest, never been near that kind of ecosystem. We realize it will be green. And wet. And warm. The coquí, little frogs of luminescent green, will sing their names all night long, calling for themselves.

I never ask the woman her name. There is something so quiet in her face that I feel it is an intrusion to know too much. I ask instead where she is going.

"To the peak. To El Yunque." Her voice sounds the soft y in *Yunque,* the word that means *white clouds* to the original Taíno people, or the sound of a giant hammer hitting an anvil to the invading Spaniards.

"The El Yunque trail, that's the path we're taking," I tell her, too chipper in my role as host. Our guidebook lists it as a four-hour hike through dense jungle. I turn to look at her in the back seat. Rum light spills from the east and highlights her strong hooked nose and angular cheekbones. She seems to make a decision.

"I will show you a better way."

How far to trust? I test the waters. "So you come here often."

"I used to come more often, but now my farm keeps me away."

"A farm? What kind of farming?" My interest in dirt flares back to childhood.

Again, silence. Then, "Flowers."

I am delighted. "Cut or nursery?"

"I grow tropical plants, and some flowers for cutting." She pauses.

I rush the silence. "So you're taking a holiday?"

"No." She looks out the window. "I come once a year to make thanksgiving."

I wait for more, but she does not explain. I am not nosy, but her silences are filled with words she is not saying. And to me, to run into a farmer in this densely populated and often urban island seems fortuitous.

I ask about water. Where it comes from, how water is used in the area. This is not idle talk. In Michigan, water is a political issue because we have much of it and the rest of the country does not. Where it goes is important, even in the north, where it's plentiful.

"Water comes from El Yunque," she says with a smile.

"But when you live here, is it a municipal system, or is it shipped from somewhere else?" One of these had to exist in a place with four million people.

"It comes from El Yunque," she says pointedly.

"All of it?"

"El Yunque makes our water."

"No, where does your farm water come from?" I ask, thinking her eyes are too dark, wondering if she has irises at all.

She smiles patiently. "It comes from the stream that comes from the mountain."

"Your water comes from a stream from the mountain? You mean from El Yunque?"

She nods, "You will see." She makes the gesture of drinking from a cup.

III. SACRED MEMORY

On our first day on the island, we discover the El Yunque Visitors' Center, a perfectly modern interactive site, and learn the basics about the rain forest, about its ecosystem, how it controls much of the climate of the entire island. As a trial run, we take a popular hike on the short but slippery Arboles Grandes (The Big Trees) to La Mina Falls.

We walk through jungle.

Here is a word embodied in its place. There on the steep and unstable slopes of the Lugillo Mountains, the jungle forms impenetrable landscapes of interlaced greenery. Mists rise spontaneously in gorges thick with Sierra palms, tabonuco, tree ferns, and plant life I cannot name. We stare, our eyes filling up with orchids and blooms that offer—besides their red, orange, purple—an interior light. Sun-starved as we are, it seems to our eyes that a radiance saturates the stone-lined paths. Succulents and huge broad-leafed palms tunnel light over giant versions of our houseplants—*Oh, this is what they're supposed to look like.* And off the paths, luxuriant complexity, leaf layers like thick pages; if you could walk into it at all, you would lose yourself, not just your physical self, but your *self,* in a hundred shades of green.

The jungle would take you.

In that awareness, we walk a careful mile over the sturdy

paths (constructed decades previously by the Civilian Conservation Corps) to the falls, La Mina—the place of cleansing—a cascade of green silk, narrow and rocky at the top, sheering into spray like silver hair over boulders to a broad pool cradled in a grotto formation. The silty river falls here in light, dreamy cream. Not just cloudy, the water looks as though it has clouds in it, touched with the lighter translucence of green.

A sturdy bridge crosses the river where the natural dam overflows and pours again down the mountain. Here, weighty with warmth, the mist clings to our hair, skin. Bright patches of mosses salted with glimmering dew soften the boulders surrounding the pool. Pattern-leafed plants and lianas lean toward the spray. The light is everywhere filtered. Every plant touches every plant near it, and everything is touched by water in this place where it might rain four times a day. Though it is early, other people have also gathered. Droplets of fine mist saturate our hair with tiny clear pearls.

A sliver. A shadow. The palm of a hand.

We watch a teenaged boy slip off the path near the bridge and hop, rock to rock, around the rim of the pool to the cascade. He lowers himself into the shallows, and it comes to me, sacred memory, how on my father's farm, the streams in the open land of the back forty pasture were fed by springs in a lush cedar swamp. That water was dark and tannic.

I remember how we dammed one of the streams in order to catch crayfish. Where we stopped the flow with an old log and stones, a tiny spill. *A waterfall*, we announced proudly to each other. Beneath that spill, in the muddy sand, there too had formed a small pool where two children could sit in the cool silt and watch the water pour over the slick stones. We could cup our hands under the spill and let the plum-colored water pour into our palms. Without much consciousness, I loved the

low unwords of streams, loved the sensation of *creek* flowing
into the hollow of my palms. I was amazed at the whisper of
night the water held. I knew the flow came from the cedar
swamp, but not the why of this necessary darkness, shadow
water.

After slipping over the stones, the boy at La Mina cannot simply settle under the falls, letting this warm green water cascade down his back, flatten his thick curls. He scrambles up
the rocks, slipping twice but catching himself and grinning
at the gasps of the watchers—for now, all eyes are turned to
him—until he stands on a narrow precipice near the brink
where the water spills. He thinks he will dive into the water directly beneath the falls, or jump in and tumble down the rocks.
A handful of young Puerto Rican men on the bridge heckle
him, but his father, an older man of Scandinavian coloring,
shouts in a distinct New York accent for him to come down.
The boy stares stonily into the pool, listening to the call, assessing its depth. The pool is seductive in its intimacy, and the
boy is swayed also by the warm lure of defiance, the embrace
of an attention-getting dive. But the rocks beneath the surface
are irregular and sharp. The sound of the waterfall seems to
grow louder with each moment he stands deciding. Then he
stretches his hands toward the rush of water, lets the green
glaze his palms. He feels *river,* he feels *waterfall.*

Will it be enough?

After he descends the rocks and wades back, his father offers his own hand, but the young man refuses him and makes
his way clumsily around his father's arm to find his way up to
the path alone.

I think about how the boy moved around that outstretched
hand, exerting his independence, rejecting authority even as

his exit from the pool acknowledged his fathers' warning. Though the pool is laced with the allure of tropical beauty, to dive its waters so far from the highway would have been foolhardy. Smart boy. He understood that. But I understand his defiance. My siblings and I piled rocks in the stream in part to catch crayfish, but also because our father had forbidden it. If any of our little dams had ever succeeded, we could have flooded the pasture.

I scramble down a narrow groove of rock that winds its way around the edge of La Mina's pool. I reach out so the spray can fall onto my hands. It glances off my palms, rolls down my arms, streaming off my skin. The jungle holds and releases, but the flow is always there, moving from one inner place—a childhood creek on a far northern farm—to another—a waterfall in a tropical forest—connection echoing in the hollow of my palms.

IV. THE BLUE BEAD

We are the water planet. From space, we look blue shot through with cream, because of the water and clouds.

A beautiful blue bead.

This time it is the bracelet of lapis beads.

Whenever I go to a new place, I lose something. In Oklahoma, it was a pashmina print shawl. In Tennessee, a favorite red windbreaker. Over time, I have developed a rationale: It is as though the places I visit need a tariff. The place will give me something, but I must pay something. This time it is a lovely bracelet of small blue planets with a silvery magnetic clasp. It's unusual for me to wear jewelry hiking, but I wore this bracelet to dinner the evening before, because it matched the intense colors of the island, because it felt festive to wear something pretty in Puerto Rico. I forgot to take it off. On the way out of La Mina, I am moving quickly, exhilarated by that first short hike. I almost hear the tumbled ticking that is not raindrops against rock, but I am caught in the falls' cleansing. It isn't till late that night, waking from a green dream in our tiny guest-house, that I remember that falling sound, separate it from the sound of the falls, touch my wrist and find it bare. I know then. I have paid.

Still, I always feel the loss.

The sun is blocked by a thick warm mist when we pull into the parking lot of the falls for the second time. The woman in the back seat tells me this is the wrong trailhead.

I nod. "Yes, we'll just take a minute. I lost something on our hike to the falls yesterday." It is a ritual process, to go back to the place where the bargain was struck. The places always look as if nothing has happened.

"What is it you lost?" she asks.

"A bracelet."

"Too bad. I will help." She jumps out, quick and lithe. I notice how muscled she is for her tiny frame. We cover the lot, paying close attention to the transition where the path spills into the parking area. The bracelet is not to be found, but she keeps looking, scanning the red and yellow clay at the edge where the tar surface ends and cracks off.

"Yesterday it rained hard on this side of the mountain. The lapis might have been washed off the tar, down here." She tells me as she bends closer to the broken asphalt. I can tell she would like to find this thing for me. Finally I touch her elbow. "It's okay. It happens to me sometimes."

"But you like this bracelet?" She says the word in Spanish, *bra-ce-la-te*, with gravity.

"I think the mountain took it."

She smiles broadly then and climbs back into the car. As the car labors up the mountain, the flora shifts again from the defined trees of Southern gardens to the denser amalgamations of cloud forest palm and epiphytes and vines that coexist in the more diverse rain forest. Sunlight fades and rises, interjected with fog and mist. Vistas open right, left, slip down the mountain, close abruptly behind a white curtain. The lushness—despite its overuse, the only word that works—becomes more so.

I finger my empty wrist . . . in gratitude.

This island is called a paradise, an enchanted isle, in spite of the abuse of industry and overpopulation. These singular tropical mountainsides exist an hour from San Juan, one of the most densely populated cities in the U.S. and its territories. As our small Brio grinds up the steep road, I wonder, is this island like Eden, its dirt and water and rock having shaped us? Gary Snyder writes about how land makes our bodies, playing the role of a god: creation to be thankful for, as the woman in the back seat is. This is the blue planet. The water planet. A bead in space. A gift. Pay the tariff.

I grew up among farmers. I know weather is one of the great forces, a god of sorts. Rain is its embodiment. I ask the woman about the weather.

"It rained on my farm," shaking her head. "All morning."

Is it the rainy season?

"In May and a part of June, and then again in October toward December. But you know, things are different. This should be the forty days without rain. We always have the forty days without rain some time between the hurricanes and the spring rainy season, but this time, there is rain all the time, much more rain. Only a few days between each rain. El

Yunque is giving us more, but it may not be good. The climate is not like that. We have regular weather for as long as we have El Yunque. Now something is not the same." Her face looks over the edge of a rich green bluff. We go quiet. What does it mean when the god shifts demeanor?

I want to ask more, yet her sense of privacy, like the jungle itself, surrounds her. I hesitate and then ask where she is from. A long pause. Have I given offense? But she answers, "I was born in Trieste, Italy, but I spent my youth in Mexico and many years ago moved here to be with a man. He moved on. I stayed with the farm." She smiles at this.

She tells us to watch the kilometer markers. At thirteen, she scans for a narrow side road, finds it, directs us off the highway. We bump along to a place where the road has been blocked by a rusty guardrail spanned with lianas and palms. We park, unfold ourselves from the small Brio. She points out a trailhead that will take us to Mount Britton. Looking over our damp map, she touches three places, "Go there. Climb the tower. Then if you want, take the side trail." She points to an unmarked peak. "It leads here." She offers a few key details. The rain begins again, determined to fulfill its two-hundred-plus inches of annual rainfall. She pulls a coral rain slicker from her daypack, slips it over her canvas jacket. She waves and walks into the jungle, her stride long for someone so small. I watch until the bright coral disappears into the green. I do not expect to see our hitchhiker again, but I feel she is more than a chance guide. We do not choose our spirit guides or our real ones. They are given to us in return for some small, inadequate gesture or wish. A gift.

With the rain, the chorus of coquí rises, calling for itself.

We walk hunched, in part because we are conscious of the overlap of palms draped just above our heads, weighted with rain that randomly spills down our necks, but also to watch our feet, testing the wet trail, which, though mostly slabbed and sometimes paved, is slippery with moss. The path becomes cave-like, pierced by light slivers and mere slips of view that reveal mist streaming off the steep mountainsides. The coquí chorus is interrupted by a duet. I find them, each perched on a scarlet spray of bird-of-paradise, two small birds with orange throats fiercely singing of love or territory. *Tody*, my book calls them. I remember that in birding, one is not supposed to point, that birds are oblivious to the human voice if soft, but point at them, and they take flight. Motion is more dangerous than sound. Without using my hands, I manage to explain to David where to find them in the branches. They let us watch for a long time.

Like a seduction, this underworld pulls away its veils. Distance becomes immediate. Except for the slim tease of long views through the undergrowth, everything is a close-up. We discover the brown and gray fist-sized snails, hear tiny lizards rustling—their presence a dryness in the damp. Once, we spot a lizard clinging to yellowed palm leaf, one large eye extending for a sidelong, skeptical look before she darts down the spine of her old frond to safety. A brown snake, coiled tightly, half dozes on a rock shelf where a little river of air brushes past his twitching tongue—his only moving part. Is he tasting the air, drinking from it? The almost-owl hoot of the ruddy quail-dove offers a call I might have answered in the deep winter of Michigan. A single bright-olive coquí, only an inch long, inflates his throat to make his name, then confirms his reputation for shyness and slips, secretive or self-conscious, underneath a coleus and disappears. The rain deepens, infusing midday with jade twilight. We pull parkas from daypacks, eschew our single umbrella as too clumsy in this low-leafed arcade. We ford small streams draped with emerald moss and slosh through a thin wash over rocks, as though we walked on water. I feel inundated, liquid, not so much drenched as permeated and fluid. The mountains-and-water sutra says, "Walking beyond and walking within are both done on water."

V. WALKING BEYOND; WALKING WITHIN

And if we are shaped by landscapes, interior or otherwise, perhaps our architecture is as well. In El Yunque, three medieval-looking stone towers rise from the jungle floor. One is on Mount Britton, one of the peaks with access from the trail we are hiking. Made of native rock two feet thick by the folks on the Works Progress Administration, these towers, with their narrow windows and spiraling interior stairs, are relatives to our Great Lakes lighthouses. These towers, too, are designed to withstand the extremes of weather, in this case hurricanes. But instead of the white stucco or red brick that characterizes northern lighthouses, their cut-stone bulk rises like the fortresses of the European castles that may have inspired them—fierce, protective. They will take the attack of wind from any direction and never give purchase. This stone architecture hunkers down against the storm as opposed to holding up the light in the storm. Gravity verses levity.

But why are they here?

After the rain's slow but constant motion, the base of the tower seems still and implacable. The tower stones rise directly out of the soil, without preamble. We traipse around the rough base to find the low entry framed by smaller, more finely cut stones with a single-rock lintel. It's dark but inviting in there. Maybe dry. We glance at each other, smiling. Here is something of childhood: the lost adventure, the stuff of fairy

tales. But when we step into the murky hollow, the keep's interior walls rise like a silo, slick with mold, pocked with rot
and falling stucco, gloomy with cold. Air chilled and dank as
a stale refrigerator. Tentatively, I touch the rusted railing, and
my fingertips come away freckled with peeling paint. We step
onto the slippery iron stairs, listening to our hollow dripping
footsteps clang and echo as we climb the long spiral. I imagine
one of Tolkien's demons using this as lair, swooping in to find
us trespassing.

A few steps from the parapet we hear the wind; the atmosphere freshens with the scent of green again and—what is
it—the rush of the demon's wings? We step into wind inundated with fog. This is not a slow gather-and-roll fog but a
translucent one carried by a near-gale. I reach for the stone
wall to steady myself as this wet restlessness pushes against
us. We feel the Braille of air; the tactile force presses our wind-
breakers against our bodies.

This tempest was going on above our heads? It takes a minute to understand.

This jungle, an epidermis of quickly growing vital greenery, is rinsed and cleansed by a second layer, the action of Caribbean westerlies. I remember that Hurricane Hugo's winds
ranged up to and over 150 miles per hour. There are those
who say that El Yunque took the brunt for Puerto Rico, that
only these mountains could modulate Hugo's force, and the
jungle, ripped and sheared as it was, gave the wind something
to chew on. Despite the damage throughout the island and to
the jungle itself, it resurrected itself. We stand in touch with
its fierce resistance, exhilarated and energized because the air
that springs against us is fast *and warm,* contrary to our northern experience of March, where wind means cold. Here, it
feels like an air bath.

Another couple puff out onto the platform from the tower stairs. We wait for them to adjust to the light, though they seem less surprised than we were. We nod, and I ask the young man if it is ever clear. He answers with a trace of condescension, "It is a rain forest. It rains. Only about thirty clear days a year. If you get a clear day, you are lucky. Mostly you just get moments."

As if on cue, the roiling air opens briefly, and the jungle below spreads out in a fall of tropical textures. I see the path we climbed, the sinewy dip in vegetation where it winds on to another peak in the distance, cloud forest and, beyond, a glimpse of the sea. Then it closes. Oh. The tower is the place where, for a brief moment, one can rise above the jungle's intensity and, if one is lucky, gain perspective. The towers are not guides to lead one to safety as lighthouses do on our inland seas; instead they rise above the dense shade of frond and vine to give bearings. They are a means to surface and locate. They are a way to map the interior for those traveling the interior. How else would I know where I am when on the ground I can see only what is close-up?

So what kind of bearings can one find where life is so thick it overgrows the meager paths humans have created? How much can we know of our geological or, for that matter, interior topography if we are given only thirty clear days a year? To gain perspective, to place a map of a jungle in one's head, a body needs a tower.

And maybe, in the lovely tension between short sight and long sight, we find the place where we learn to see both views.

VI. TULIP

Down on the path, we reenter the green tunnels and head for

the unmarked peak using the side path that our hitchhiker indicated. I ask David what we should call her, this woman on
her thanksgiving pilgrimage.

"Hmm. Tulip."

"Tulips don't grow here."

He points to the tulip tree, its sunset blossoms rising above
the cool hillside textures. Sometimes we pass under one, where
the coral and caramel blossoms dot the forest floor like pretty
scraps.

He points. "It's like her raincoat."

Tulip it is.

After that, we don't speak much. We work the climb,
avoiding slippery spots, leaping streams. In a marriage as old
as ours, there are three ways of making conversation: One is
the comfortable, everyday talk of what has been done, what
needs to be organized, accomplished, carried out. It is the talk
of dishes and duties, of woodsheds and order. Another is the
deep intense talk of realization and acknowledgment. This is
the middle-of-the-night waking dream before sex, the long talk
in the car after five hours at the family reunion. The third is
silence. The easy silence of two people who are tuned to each
other. It is a rich silence, often filled with imagined conversa-
tions. It does not matter whether they have been articulated or
not; it is as if they have happened. This is the silence, punctuated by coquí and birdcall, in which we walk.

I am imagining how to tell David that I will write about
this. I imagine I have a cup of coffee, and it is morning in the
north country. I am trying to describe to him what he's already
seen, the verdure—I will use that word and then discard it—in
a way that he will nod and say things back to me that I have
forgotten but once he says them I will remember always. He is
my first audience, and even as we hike, my jacket now soaked

through, I am beginning to let the jungle shape my language.

Then we find her.

We have been climbing for a long time into the upper reaches of these mountains. These mountains are not high, barely three thousand feet above sea level, but the suddenness of their rise from sea level makes them notable and, in the final ascent, steep. Our last marker tells us that we are still quite far from El Yunque's peak, but the terrain map indicates this smaller peak, nearly as tall. The footpath—a smaller trail veering off the main trail—though narrow and faded, is identifiable. This is the peak Tulip indicated before she forged ahead. By now we are sweating, chilled, and undeniably tired, but we turn off and climb again. The air seems syrupy with what we now recognize as the characteristic mix of fog, mist, wind all punctuated by *Ko-kee? Are you me?*

The jungle thins along this trail, appears lower, almost stunted. We are moving into elfin forest. Here, because of constant wind, thin soil, and heavy rains, the foliage literally shortens and can no longer hide the steep spine of this ridge. Both sides fall off so quickly that I can touch the canopy by simply reaching out my arms. We come out of this lower tangle into wind again. We are about half way up a broken slope going somewhere I cannot yet see when I stop, unsure. If either of us slipped . . .

The wind rises, whispers *risk, risk* at the mist, which clears before us.

We see her then.

The rock formation is a giant's balding head, fringed with elfin flora, rising from the cascade of jungle that surrounds it. The path toward it levels for a brief length, then a final short scramble, and the peak rounds into the air, an outcropping flattened just enough for a person to sit on it. Tulip is there, cross-legged on a folded blanket. Her coral rain cape is tucked around her, a wind-fluttered pulse. Her hood is pulled over her dark hair, and she could be an enormous flower but for her face in profile. She is staring south, her eyes intent and calm. The wind thrashes around her, but the fog is so thick that she seems suspended in a private maelstrom: the rock an island within the island of Puerto Rico, and she is the calm center.

The winds pushes and releases.

We edge along the path, closer to her rock. Where the path ends, we sit, climb no further. We can see her clearly from here. She sits immobile, as if this wind does not exist, or as if it were lover's breath, and she has turned toward it. She watches the mist. Reading it? Breathing into it? The moving dampness swirls around us. I close my eyes. After a while this mesmerizing wind warms me.

As though she knew we were there all along, she turns her head, calls down to us, "Watch now." Like a developing photograph revealing itself or ghosts becoming visible, the view appears. For the second time that day, we gradually make out the canyon depths around us, but larger than before, majestic swales and slopes folding and unfolding. She points to now-visible crevasses where the water launches over bluffs and sluices down volcanic fault lines, using these rock channels as natural chutes to the gorges. We can see falls flicker, streams as ribbons of mist uncoiling from clefts, signaling their corridors. Between shredded clouds, the far mountains, a whole spine of peaks running west, firm as warriors. And then—a thing opposite of the usual—mist rising rather than falling, rising from the depths of the valleys on the warm drafts. This mist runnels vertically, carried on some swift updraft Tulip must have seen far below. It lifts and lifts again, multiple layers rising like long shawls torn and stretched parallel to the slope of the mountain, rising high into a momentary blue, swirling into themselves.

This is not like seeing serene clouds wrapping a mountain. These mists are rising with purpose, levitating from the gorges, flowing like reversed rivers. They are coming from the green and tangled mesh that is the mountain's arteries, its skin. The mists lift like bioluminescent vapor, a living chiffon, higher than the peak of the mountain.

They thicken, become tangible, then opaque.

Oh. Oh.

This is the rain forest making a cloud.

This is cloud-making

This is the mountain making rain.

This is the jungle feeding itself.

This is how water is done.

Then the view closes, and we are in it. Not just inside mist, but in the cloud, the tug and roil of molecular spirit.

Rain.

This is why it feels so alive here.

Is this what it means to walk within water? To understand its motion and meaning inside and outside so deeply that it feels miraculous? All around me, Tulip's thanksgiving. I breathe it in, let it go. Present. I look at David. He is here, too. He nods and stays still, always more able than I am to live what is.

We sit with her for—I don't know how long—and then, without saying a word, it is as though she or the mountain dismiss us. They have their work to do; we should let them be. Simultaneously, we both feel the cold. We rise and turn and pick our way down the rough path. We leave this woman of the coral cape, this woman who reveals rainmaking. We walk down the path. There is nothing we can say for a long time. When we speak, we speak ordinary concerns.

Are you cold?

Do you need water?

Do you need to rest?

The words seem tender, as though they were from the third language of marriage, the one of silence. Everything . . . heightened. We keep walking through the streams. Or is it that they are walking through us? We find a rock that appears to have petroglyphs on it. We trace them with our fingers, catching island mud under our fingernails. I remember that petroglyphs were often carved to mark the grave of a child. Since I can't tell for sure, I imagine these markings mean the world will live, something I have doubted.

We strive for the third peak, El Yunque itself. We climb and drop and climb through the now familiar chartreuse light. The last hundred yards link to the end of an old paved road in ill repair. In a strange twist, this peak is topped with communications towers and all the apparatus that goes with them. We trudge past this modern ruin to the ruins of a small church with views to the seas on both sides. No door remains, but there is an empty fireplace with two small benches built on each side. A chipped Greek cross graces the chimney in faded orange mosaic. Windows, latticed here and there with lead, have no glass. We eat cheese and almonds, drink the last of our water. We rest here and listen to the hallowed voice rail against the stuccoed walls. Even here, in this abandoned symbol of Christianity, atop the highest peak, the spirit of the place is permeated with El Yunque. *I am here,* the jungle, the mountain, the wind say, identifying themselves in the face of the cut stone and mosaic. *I will stay.*

VII. PERSEPHONE

As we are leaving the church, we meet an old man, a worker
for the park, walking along the old road. He has folded a broad
leaf into a cone-shaped cup, and he is collecting berries. He has
many in his cup. I don't recognize them. He offers me some.
I hesitate, he smiles, lifts the leaf cup like a chalice. I raise one
finger, my index finger. He makes a motion to pour them into
my hand. When I open my palm, he pours into it four berries.
He does the same for David. In another language, he tells us
they are *fresa,* a strawberry, sour and plump with juice. Red,
with a white-and-coral center.

   We eat them. He laughs, waves, disappears into the understory.

   Now we have eaten the pomegranate seeds. El Yunque has
struck a bargain with us, and we must now always return here,
to the upper world. A string of blue beads and a woman like a
flower. The tart taste of berries. The call of the coquí, naming:
You. Me. The touch of sacred clouds. The mountain of water.
Now it walks beside me, inside me, through me. Thanksgiving.

> In our dream of safety, we decided not to know the world.
>
> *Jim Harrison*

Edge of Possibility

Santa Monica, California

It is the second year of the war. He sits on the plank steps, his face covered with sweat, and he is bent over his belly like a woman with cramps, knees almost to a squat. He is making sounds that do not seem to be words but something like words. It takes me a long time to realize he is crying, not just slippery tears down his face, but long sobs, like a slow wave coming in and going out with every breath.

At 7:00 a.m., the door of the hotel on Santa Monica's main drag swings softly behind me, separating the cool, center-pieced interior from the sunny, raucous exterior. I'm thrust onto the bright morning sidewalk, out into the February street, where the soft, cool air prophesies the day's warmth, nothing at all like the frigid temperatures I've left in Michigan, where we will struggle with winter for two more months. Traffic is awake and humming with engines: SUVs and sports cars, travel buses and limousines. Despite the activity and bustle that is a California city street, I take this cherished morning walk before I launch into a day where I will represent, along with several other instructors and administrators, my beloved Interlochen Arts Academy.

We are here to promote the new film department for gifted young filmmakers. I am happy to do the work, happy to have been invited, happy to talk to people about an education I believe in. That said, by nature I need some solitude every day. And because there is no snow and no cold, because there exists a large ocean and wide park and the Santa Monica pier just down this busy street, I will take this early hour before the day to walk alone.

Except I am not alone. A large portion of Santa Monica's population honor the same impulse. Hundreds of people run, jog, skate, and walk in this park. Dressed in American sportswear marked with bold insignia, we do the dance of exercise. In designer shorts and shirts we show off every muscle and tattoo as though we were action figures. If we'll admit to aches and pains, even to sweat, we mask them with rainbow-colored joint braces and emblemed headbands. One woman speed-dances past me on iridescent purple skates that might cost me a month's salary.

My pace is middle-aged reasonable as I pass glassy hotels and well-appointed apartment buildings in this wealthy district where we're housed, where more tourists, business people, and families pour out of these chrome-and-tinted-glass doors, all headed for the park and pier. At the nearest light, I see for the first time traffic lights that count down seconds remaining in crossing time—an eerie warning that we should not be caught crossing with no seconds left. People jog in place, watching the numbers change. A few touch the throbbing vein at their throats and check their watches. A few just touch their watches; they already know their pulses.

As I cross into the park proper, I concentrate on not bumping into anyone on the paths as I adjust my own tempo, weaving in and out of moving bodies and madrone shadows. I adapt to the panting throngs, move briskly to that pace where I am accelerating my heart rate but am still able to observe. Even in winter, the park blooms. Beside the spreading oak, bird-of-paradise send up their bright yelp, yucca grow the size of spiky sailboats, succulents and palms rise in stately formation. There are plumes of bougainvillea and a trailing blossom I cannot name that tucks back in the shade.

Is that when I see them?

There, among the trees and shrubbery, near public bathrooms and along the benches, they push carts or shuffle or sit. Not one or two, but more than I have ever seen congregated in my travels in Chicago, New York, or Washington. They are waking, too. In contrast to the energetic exercisers, they move as though a measured dance of communal motion were being established, and they are the slow gestures that give perspective to how fast everything else is moving. Some drink coffee from gnawed Styrofoam cups, some sort their overflowing carts, some already trudge down the streets with their backpacks trailing plastic sacks, some still lie wrapped in sleeping bags under the trees. A distrust I recognize as fear pokes its head through the weave of my perceptions. Here in one of the wealthiest shoreline districts around Los Angeles, I would like to be a Pollyanna about my safety, but caution rises in me.

They could be dangerous.

As I'm having this battle, I hear the small rhythm of morning greetings move back and forth from the people in the shadows to the sports folk, the runners and skaters.

Hey, Sam, how are ya this mornin'?

Mornin', Mr. Man, what's the buzz?

Cookin'. How are you, Hank?

Bad teeth, bad coffee. Couldn't be better.

Howdy, howdy, howdy, howdy, howdy.

Back at ya.

Laced with slang, slur, obsessive repetition, or with the clipped, metallic enunciation of success, greetings slip from shadow to the breathless sun and back again, from the low benches with a slow wave to Mr. Man on the run and back to *howdyhowdyhowdy*. The litany of phrases takes on a ceremonial quality that dispels my suspicion. I take the cue and let my fear go. Whether the bodies be dressed in fashion-plate lycra or old camo, I meet their eyes and dare a nod. I walk freely the short mile to the corner where the foot of the Santa Monica pier is spanned by a wide carnival arch. I pass under and walk out to face the spacious Pacific.

For everyone else the pier is a tacky tourist strip of carnie-style kiosks selling shell toys and souvenir spoons made in China—but for me, with a midwesterner's love of festival and fairs, the best part of the walk is the pier.

I am in California for heaven's sake, what's a little tack?

That night, after meetings with Hollywood folks about the film-studies project, we sit, dazed and delighted, in a four-star restaurant, perusing a menu the size of a family bible. I order what my sophisticated boss orders, lobster bisque, because he knows what's good. The conversation moves back and forth from the personalities we encountered to the promise of these relationships for the school. I shift in the brocade seat, sip the delicious California Chardonnay. Some alums with us are from L.A., one couple from Santa Monica. They ask about our accommodations. *Fine, fine.* We compare the weather here to the weather in Michigan, always good for a gasp and a couple of "how cold it gets" stories. The talk is light and full of good humor.

I ask about the people in the park.

They are not unwilling to talk, but are cautious about this tricky subject. They know a little. I learn the park people are mostly men, many vets. The Santa Monica couple have heard a hierarchy exists among the homeless there, and there are leaders among them who keep a kind of rule. Not just anyone can stay in this park, though some do stay year round, depending on the cops and the purpose they keep. I tell them about the greetings among the park people. They seem pleased by this, nod, *Yes, that's probably it,* people know each other after all this time. They speak of human service programs, assistance plans.

I look around the table. The lighting is soft. We all look fine in our strappy summer dresses, our light jackets. The day has gone well with the movie people. There will be an advisory board, perhaps donations of equipment. We order after-dinner liqueurs and toast our success, and I do not ask any more questions.

By the third time I walk, I recognize certain people—the woman with the blue umbrella sticking out of her grocery cart, the man with the red backpack—but I can't ascertain a leader. But how could I, a middle-aged, rural white woman with a bad hip and a worn pair of New Balance? What could I possibly know of their lives, of the world they live in? I feel ashamed of my curiosity, my objectification. I try to be more respectful. What I see, if I look past all the complications of my cultural bigotry, is that they hold themselves, even here in this public forum, in a small frame of privacy. I suspect there is a hard peace among them, but I cannot know the elements of its treaty.

I don't push my thinking further. I walk out each morning through the park and down to the end of the pier. I concentrate on the walk, on getting to the pier, hitting the boards, and striding to the end where the air freshens off this Pacific Ocean, the ocean named for peace. As the week progresses, people begin to recognize me on the planked wooden pier. I greet the venders as they set up their kiosks and tables in the cool morning light. They nod back. One who is surrounded by grimy Styrofoam coolers asks me, *You fishin'? You want bait?*

Here is the world come to sell: a family tossing acrylic shawls and macramé necklaces with pine-cone amulets over wobbling chrome racks; a man in a wheelchair cleverly pushing an attached cart loaded with tiny Ferris wheel replicas inside glass globes shuddering with glitter; Asian painters who will, for a fee, write my name in a fancy scarlet and chartreuse script.

No Oceana County fair of my youth can match this.

Halfway down the pier, a set of steps interrupts the railing and leads down to the north, to a wide beach below Santa Monica. Twice I cut down to the shore, crossing the sand to watch the waves roll in the long slow rush, hitting the sand in a high tinkling shush. Once, a seal swims playfully close. The black-marble eyes look right at me, and then she flips and I get just a quick slice of her sleek back. A circle of men gather on the sand, some in low chairs. They speak and nod, then go quiet, and then the low tones rattle again in soft exchange. Are they a support group, a bible study come to pray together, an early AA meeting? Or just a group of men gathered to talk— though it seems too deliberate for that. I notice the man with a camo jacket gesturing animatedly, and several others lean forward.

I remind myself I cannot know their stories.

I head back to the wooden pier, climb the stairs, turn oceanward to the pier's end, where the coast guard building perches on the final stretch, surrounded by a wide, bi-level deck. The bathrooms and snack bar are tucked here, facing the shore, and for most people, that meets their needs. But on the far side, a surprise. More wooden steps lead down to the lower level of the deck that looks directly out onto the Pacific. Here, low gray bleachers buffer the bustle of the rest of the pier.

Here, I am among the fisher people.

Apparently they come from all over the world to set up their bait buckets at the end of this famous dock. They open their coolers and bait their lines and cast out over the deep green water that stretches all the way to Japan. Men and women lean against the sea barriers and stare and sometimes smoke. Their words move over the air, rarely loud and always in the ordinary language of people at a task. Spanish and Eastern languages mingle with broken English—though they all seem to understand each other. One old man speaks something that might be Arabic, and the frowsy woman in the rumpled blue shirt answers in Spanglish, and they laugh as though they have shared a very good joke. They nod to me and sometimes greet me, but mostly I am the woman with the small notebook who sits awhile on the steps, who stares at slow swells, then at her pages. If they mind my presence, they are too courteous to let me know.

Once, when we are nearly finished with our work for Interlochen, I come to the pier at sunset. All my life, I have watched sunsets. The Michigan farmhouse where I grew up faced west, and the sun's low-angled golds spilled over the western hill and flooded our dining room. In college, I belonged to the Sunset Club. We used precious gas money to drive to Lake Michigan, where we would rank numerically sunsets according to clarity, color, and an amorphous quality we called "drama." *That's a ten. Naw, not enough variation. It's only an eight. Well, eight and a half.*

This evening, my friends and colleagues wander among the kiosks, but I walk to the end of the pier and lean over the last railing to watch. The sun shifts in a wild incarnadine sea that in any other setting would be gaudy, but with the backdrop of carnival is a composition in the heated colors of the world. The scarlet clouds on the horizon hold voluptuous pink frills. The sky is crimson-ornate and bedecked as a full-bodied woman in orange boas and pastel mares' tails. Beneath her, the heavy ocean darkens, glazed with a promenade of gold. A ten.

I lean over and stare into the darkness. Here, too, is our final boundary, a liquid precipice—here the completion of manifest destiny; here at last, after all the rampant thrusting miles over sand and rock, river and mountain, all that endless possibility dropped into an abyss of light and sea. Here, the future changed its nature, could change it again.

Other people gather to watch as our small earth angles away from its star. Sometimes there is one who looks as though he sees something other than color, sees the drama. They light cigarettes and flick ash toward the pilings; they lean forward with their wrists draped over the metal rails and gorge on this and do not talk, not even the ordinary unimportant talk, about the abandon and abandonment of light.

The man does not put his hands to his face, except now and then to chew the cuff of his camo jacket. He has cried so long that there is a ring of clean around his eyes, nose, and mouth, but the rest of his face is shiny with grime.

The last day. Sunday morning in California's fair February. A far-seeing sky. Good air. Because I don't have meetings and my plane doesn't leave until afternoon, I walk later than usual. Once on the street, I realize there are fewer runners. Sunday is a sleep-in morning, a recovering-from-Saturday-night-morning, or a family morning. But because there are fewer bright runners to balance the presence of the homeless, it is hard not to notice, at first only in small ways, that something is awry.

Directly across the street from the hotel, the woman with the blue umbrella races her cart quickly back and forth between two poles. She swings the cart one way and runs into the pole and then yanks it away again and races back at the first. She crashes into the pole, or misses it and swings around as though it were a pivot. I pass that corner and head for the next light. But there under the *ten, nine, eight* a thin man in tattered pants and a T-shirt shouts at a man twice his size. They raise their arms, point fingers, lumber at each other.

As I move down the blocks, the undercurrent of sound that accompanies a city shifts, divides, becomes distinct voices. The affable language of previous mornings has been replaced with the mutterings and gutturals of some ripped-open emotion. *Mofucka, sonabitch, dogsass.* If I had stood still in that moment, I would have found the harsh rhythms of aggression beautiful—a growl of storm with profanity as its refrain. But I can't separate the tension from its sound: where are the pleasantries that, however superficially, signaled safety? Instead, the communal snarl snakes under the trees, crouches on the hoods of cars, hovers on charred wings. Contradiction rules; on a bright and peaceful morning, the language is night language, smog words and glass-splintered sentences.

All the way to the pier, I stay on the city side of the street, walking with my invisible face on, but paying attention to what is happening in the park across the street. They are awake, but cantankerousness runs like a river among these people who on other mornings seem to rise as sleepily as I do. Before long, three police cars begin a slow cruise up and down the highway. They roll along the park side, and because I am watching them, walking on the opposite side of the street, because I am thinking it all must have something to do with Saturday night, I do not see what is coming. I do not see it until I cross the street at the Santa Monica Pier arch, cross the bridge to the pier and am thudding down the gray planking. And then, halfway down, just where the open stairs slope to the sand, I see the beach.

The sound of the waves is punctuated by the soft *shusht, shusht* of the spikes at the base of each small cross as it is planted in the sand. Already the plumb lines are run, so that the rows will be straight and square. A little girl straightens each cross so the tidiness becomes a contradiction. A young man in a beret and two others in uniform thrust white crosses with that brush of percussion that sounds like a shuffling march. They carry out this work meticulously, as though this beach were a seedbed and they plant a garden and not these tiny metaphorical grave markers. It is as though these markers have to be in perfect order because that order will combat the chaos that creates the need for them at all.

Wearing their calm faces, the peace workers move up and down the grid. They smooth the sand, set stakes, run the lines,

plant the crosses, smooth again. Then the next. And the next.
One young woman carries a bundle of additional crosses
fanned in her arm like a bouquet. Row after row. Their symbolic cemetery will spread across and down the beach until
they have planted crosses representing . . . how many deaths?
Is this why the people of the park shouted at each other? Is this
what they saw? They all know what the crosses mean, and so
their fragile peace is distorted?

In this sun-drenched world, where so many of the homeless are soldiers, where their history with another war might
have contributed to their homelessness, where they have been
forgotten or left to the devices of a crumbling caretaking system, an antiwar demonstration, quiet and reverent as it is,
might remind these men and women of the deaths of their
own war. Here, the repeated image of the cross might run like
a flame on a fuse back to a moment of loss or killing or cross
fire or terrible maiming that makes one look kindly on, indeed
wish for, death. The crosses, one after another, might spark the
contradiction of honorable duty and terrible culpability.

I take the steps to the sand, drawn to this place, the work,
drawn to these activists setting up a day of mourning for the
men and women lost. At the bottom of the steps, a woman
my age hands me a small brochure that explains Veterans for
Peace, explains that they will set a white cross for every soldier
lost in this war, a red cross for every nongovernmental civilian
lost, blue for every ten people. I watch it happen, first one row
and then another, and each time one of those people sets a
cross, I feel as though I have lost everyone.

The planters are quiet but aware. As people find the demonstration, the volunteers invite them to walk among the
crosses. More gather, mostly silent, but now and then a soft
voice filters among the crosses, speaking of what is being

done. Volunteers step alongside me as though to guide me into some ceremony that they are familiar with and I am not.

The little girl who earlier was straightening crosses asks if I want water, and I wipe my face and nod.

How long do I stay there, walking among the small, orderly crosses, walking the soft sand between the rows, walking back to the staging area near the steps, where there are signs that list every date since the war began and the names of the soldiers who died on those days? Finally I hear him.

His is the face from a Bosch painting of hell, or like Michelangelo's last day, when we are all divided, and the chosen are raised and the rest of us left to despair. He is the man in the camo jacket. I have seen him in the park.

He perches on the steps like a frightened animal. I stand below him on the sand, and when I look up the stairs, I can see his face. He is holding himself in an agony I cannot fathom, except for the way we fathom our nightmares. He is leaning forward, staring at the crosses, and his mouth is open, lips twisted, and his voice is gaining volume. Now many of the others on the sand lift their heads, turn from that field to look up toward him. We see him seeing the crosses. We see him take in every one of them, those planted and those still to plant, and what he gives back to us is a story for each cross, trapped and encapsulated in his almost-words. We see in his streaming eyes, in his newly clean face the preamble to each of these crosses. We understand that we have seen nothing compared to what he has seen, and we see how the crosses must loom for him, the shadow of each desperate story he reads in them.

In that moment, he is every soldier. He is every survivor and witness from Iraq to Eastern Europe, from Sudan and

Darfur, right back to those wars against indigenous people in our own land. In his face is the great sorrow, the one from which we cannot turn away.

I decipher at last the sounds he is shaping with his mouth—num-bers. He is counting. But out of order. Numbers dislodged from order. Listen . . . one hundred, two hundred, sixty-seven, ninety-four, three hundred, a thousand, two, three . . . as if identifying each of the dead by number. In each sob, the body count lands randomly in a different chasm of grief, so that sixty-seven is embodied as a teenager playing checkers in the Vietnamese jungle, looking up just before a greater sound interferes. Two thousand twenty is a nurse in Operation Des-ert Storm, setting a fractured bone just before the IED tears through the medical tent.

I do not walk to the end of the pier. I cannot go any closer to the edge of the world with its brilliant abyss of possibility. I stand still, listening to the numbers, their dead-on check on all possibility. I stand in the light, in the clear heat of California, this place where so many lost vets have come—the irony of a warm climate—because it is easier to be here than anywhere else. Through the sun-ridden grief of the man's counting, I think of the crosses, their numbers mounting at my back. I think of the survivors, so often silent, uncounted, invisible.

An Elongated Tear

Culebra, Puerto Rico

Culebra is an American Virgin Island with a fierce sound for a past, a sound that still hollows it out and leaves it damaged. Culebra is full of sun and charm, but beneath that, there are the ghosts of empty shells, the whisper of the firing range, the rusted shrapnel blown over with sand. The bombs had to be tested, and they were tested here; the soldiers had to be trained, and they were trained here, on Culebra and Vieques, two tropical Caribbean islands off the eastern shore of the main island of Puerto Rico. Here the U.S. military dropped literal tons of bombs from every angle. Here they practiced on long and short firing ranges, and the ships tossed their refuse, and when they were done, there was little "nature" left, except the weather. It is still there, weather and shells. You will find the barnacled shapes of those bombs and missiles settled in the currents on the floor of the surrounding ocean. Scaled and ribboned with green weed, these elongated teardrops rest with all the guile of war, decades old, on the bottom of the sea.

In 1975, the U.S. military finally left Culebra. The western part of the island became a highly controlled nature preserve, though not necessarily out of the will to preserve—the natural flora was mostly destroyed by shelling or threatened by non-native species. Rather it was protected because there was so much unexploded ordnance, so much in the testing that had failed and that may or may not have, depending on which side is speaking, created a mysterious residual that affects the health of the island and its people. But the ordnance itself is no mystery. It can be seen, pointed to, and occasionally even deadlier evidence of its existence reverberates off the coast.

When you drop a thousand bombs, a few fail. When you drop a thousand times a thousand, trying to get it right—how to aim, how to target, how to make destruction work—how many then fail to explode?

These are the waters of Culebra.

Still, some areas were never bombed, and some have been declared clear. And we weren't thinking about ordnance the morning we didn't go to Flamingo Beach on the north side of Culebra, having heard it was one of the most beautiful beaches in the world. Even if we didn't know what "live ordnance" meant yet, we knew what "most beautiful" meant. Even on a distant island like Culebra, overcrowding occurs because it is so close to Puerto Rico. The prosperous people of the larger island sail to the smaller island to enjoy the peace and quiet, but in the process (as happens everywhere), peace and quiet packs up and leaves, and what's left is a big party.

Puerto Rican coffee is as strong as sunshine, filling David and me with the northern energy that the islanders shake their heads about. At our guest house at Villa Fulladoza, we abandon breakfast in our outdoor kitchen scattered with novels and notebooks and half-eaten toast, climb into a rented Volkswagen Thing the color of moldy butter and head, grinding gears the entire way, for Rosario, an isolated beach on the far west side of the island, tucked into a protected cove that nurtures a reef laden with tropical life.

We have come for one of my favorite worldly experiences, shallow-water snorkeling.

We park at Flamingo Beach and walk the half-mile over pitted terrain to Rosario Beach. We snorkel all morning, immersing ourselves in this alternative existence, an underwater wilderness. There, we watch a school of blue angelfish swim among hovering yellowtail, float with parrotfish and blue-striped grunts and all the tiny ones whose names I am still learning, but the sight of which are petals burned on my brain. We swim among brain coral and fan coral and delicate kitelike creatures barely visible in the golden water.

When I snorkel, my five reliable senses shift, alter their purposes. Due to the nature of the mask, smell and taste become sealed; sound is dulled to hollow signals like the clipped tap of the grunt banging its hard mouth on the coral or the distant, almost dreamlike thud of a powerboat. Sight is paradoxically narrowed through the tunnel of mask. One must turn the head deliberately, as though casting a beam. Short sight is heightened because the light, while truncating distances, seems to pierce the water so that certain colors turn golden, and others nearly disappear. My tactile sense heightens because the other senses tamp down. The warm all-over touch of water becomes super-luscious, recalls the forgotten time of swimming in the womb. We float in the contradiction of security and flying.

Gestures become words because one must use hand signals. Pointing is paramount. All is gesticulation, a clumsy charade of jabbing fingers. Look that way. The spray of weed dotted with orange. Look there. A school of yellow-striped wonder. There. Swift iridescence scooting under coral. Creatures so alarmingly lovely that I would gasp if I could. I know, suddenly surrounded by a million tiny silver arrow fish, this is where life must have begun.

We snorkel until, unbelievably in these balmy waters, we became cold, and we have to give up, swim back in, rise clumsily in our fins, and shuffle toward the warm shore, saddened to abandon dream flight.

We snorkel until the boats roll in with their throaty engines, and even this more isolated beach becomes a popular destination. Only then do we walk back over the ridge to Flamingo to brave the crowds after all, thinking they can be no worse than those invading Rosario.

I discover that Flamingo is a deceptive beach. It appears to be one thing but is another.

Traipsing across the makeshift unpaved parking area, I notice that the sand of Flamingo appears similar to the sand of the beaches along our beloved Lake Michigan, sugary and light, soft to the step. And as at many Michigan beaches, one walks over a low dune to a wide view spreading out left and right to the horizon. Flamingo is similarly elegant, a graceful horseshoe with distant points, the eastern one rocky, the western a sandy spit pointing to the reef, where the surf breaks.

At first, walking over the sand toward the water, I think, well . . . so it's true . . . there is nothing as special as my own home beach in Leelanau County. And then I hear the surf in its roll, turning in slow sleep. I near the water, and the air, always heavier in this part of the world, takes on translucence. Then the sand's texture becomes velvety cream, but firm, like walking on fine silk stretched taut. Over that sand, swirling in for hundreds of feet, waves shallow as chiffon. David takes my hand and we walk farther, and the sand is a fine palm for our tired feet, a long shivery song of sensation. Ocean scents, flower scents, mist, the envelope both clear and laden with moisture. Without thinking, we drop our gear in a pile and walk the slow walk into the shallows. We take on a dazed look because dazed we are, breathing this yielding light. That first time, we walk east a long way and then sit down and doze, tangled in each other's arms, tired from the long swim with fish, but now gentled by this beach with its warm courtesy.

Jorge is a young Adonis, slim and muscled, with long dark hair. His black eyes are bright, his voice deep, but not loud, and almost Patrician in its pronunciation of English—though he slips into Spanish effortlessly. Like so many here in these islands, he is originally from the mainland, though now settled a decade into the island culture, long enough to claim it as his home. He stands behind the small counter in his art shop and speaks softly of his friend, a poet who is being sued for speaking out against development of the island.

It is Jorge who tells us about the tanks.

Wherever we go, I seek the local art. It is not easy to find in Dewey, the main town on Culebra. Many shops import the usual mementos created by sweat labor in other lands, and though they're advertised as "handmade," they have the look of multiplication. I look for something made with local hands and local resources. I'm willing to pay a fair price for an honest piece of art, something lovely and clear that will bring memory back to me and will offer pride to the maker. After walking the streets lined with tourist shops, I find Jorge's little shop on a side street, just down from Mamacita's, our favorite bar. "Arte" is one room, open at the back to a workspace that is really a kind of tree house over a ravine. The front room is full of paintings, photographs, jewelry of Culebra's signature green stone, some hand-cut mother of pearl—I pick an amulet with seven peach pearls still imbedded in it. Jorge also sells me a hand-sewn chapbook of poems by Paul Franklin, the friend who is in trouble. The proceeds support his court case. The poems are angry rhymes with great passion hidden beneath the language of distrust.

I wander the shop, come upon a series of simple block prints on delicious paper. The print I am attracted to is enigmatic—part fish, part slim dancer, part skeleton. Its colors are dark, purple and black, set sharply on white Strathmore. I notice the pencil signature is his, Jorge Acevedo.

"Tell me about this one," I ask.

He picks it up, turns it once—it looks like a skeleton, half fish, half human. He turns it again. Now like a dancer. Again, and it becomes a diving fish. "This is my symbol for what's happening here."

He begins talking about the turtles. "They are endangered, the leatherbacks and loggerheads. Scientists are monitoring the nests."

I look at the print, trying to make the connection between the art and the turtles.

"We are the only place in the Caribbean where the sea turtles' nests are on the rise," he tells me with quiet pride.

I look at him skeptically. "And that's because . . . ?"

"Live ordnance."

I look so startled, he chuckles. "It's the only way we are protected."

I stare at his young, serious eyes.

"They are rising from the ashes like this dancer," he says. "Sea turtles, fish, even parts of the reef. We were dead, bombed to nothing, and we are coming back now, for a little while, because they do not want to touch the bombs."

He sounds like a young messiah offering a quiet sermon.

After the guns quieted, Jorge tells me, the terns returned; long after the ships withdrew, the bright fishes found habitat in the sunken ones. The waters settled, and with the military gone, the village industries, after trouble with unemployment and alleged corruption, returned to local subsistence. The tourist trade, small but energetic, grew and now, in the last few years, has developed a thriving ecotourism.

The significantly wealthy, Jorge says, are silent and withdraw to their villas overlooking the distant shores. The significantly poor squat in tin camps in the remote hills. And there are the villagers and the ordinary people who love the island, their home, and cherish its slowly returning beauty. The island planners, up until recently, have been discouraged from developing large resorts because the live ordnance is still there. The old bombs are not just in the water, but in the soil, the rocks and crevasses. Culebra and its cousin island, Vieques, are not untouched paradises; they are, rather, a jumble of destroyed and rejuvenating ecosystems held in shaky truce by a sunken, living danger. This is what, to some small degree, has kept island development in check.

In Culebra, you must always stay on the designated paths.

You must listen closely to all warnings.

The next day David and I hike down one of those barely designated trails to a north beach called Brava, *rough one*. At the makeshift trailhead, we park next to a half-finished hut with goats and a dog who barks obsessively. It's a long trek through gullied terrain. We climb a horse trail through dense thicket up over a long ridge, then down into a winding swamp.

Like Michigan, Culebra has mosquitoes and biting flies. They rise as we move through the grasses. The little lizards rustle in the underbrush; the sun comes and goes as clouds scuttle across a sky filigreed by the canopy of scrub forest. We scramble over sections of the trail washed out in spring rains, sinking now and then into a dry gulch eight feet deep. We get lost in the scrub where the trail splits and then fades. We back-track to the main trail, pass the ruins of a Spanish well centuries old, skirt a wild bee hive, cross near a stagnant lagoon graced by a pair of egrets. Finally, hot and scratching, we reach a place where the trail opens onto the beach, totally empty, which in turn opens to the wide expanse of ocean. We stash our packs against a rock shelf that offers some shadow.

We look around. We are delightfully alone except for the surf, a whale of surf. Huge and distant, the waves shape themselves far out, gathering enormous size as they roll over reef. They are so large that they seem like the giant backs of clumsy creatures shouldering slowly through the distant deeps. They are enormous, but they wheel in leisurely, breaking heavily against the long sloping arms of the beach.

This surf is not something we think about.

Because here are the cooling waters, here, translucent air laden with iridescent mist tossed up by the roll of the waves. We are hot. We want to be refreshed. We do not hesitate. We run out a spit of sand and into the water to stand in the ebb and flow.

We do not yet understand the reach of the waves, the unchecked force of Brava. We are in up to our ankles, leaping and playful. I throw my arms open, sighing at the coolness. Way out, a distant wave rises, teasing at first, washes in slowly around our calves, tasting. It rises again, enough for us to splash each other, and aren't we glad we came all that way and now we can swim? And then we are in to our thighs, and how did that happen? We didn't walk out into it; it came to us, didn't it?

We are drenched and laughing.

And then we feel it, the inner pull, the deep insistence, the weight of water against the backs of our legs and knees. It is immense. We are standing in it, only a few feet apart, laughter dying. I realize what is happening. I know, by every alerted sense in me, that it could simply take my feet out from under me and sweep me out. Rip tide such as I have never felt in my life. We look at each other, and David feels it too, and the wave is rising again. This time the sound alerts me, the mounting thrum of wave, intensifying like the inside of storm.

We have taken this place too lightly.

Suddenly I am reaching for David, who is reaching for me, and we lock hands and turn and push ourselves hard away, slipping in soft bottom-sand that pulls out from under our feet so fast we can barely keep footing, but must keep it, keep moving, stumbling, struggling out of the grip of a current stronger than anything we have ever encountered in any of our travels.

That kind of power. Brava. Rough one. Greedy one.

When we finally get clear, I stand well up on the beach with my arms crossed, holding myself and gasping, *oh my god, oh my god,* astonished at how close we have come to disappear-

ance. David shakes his head, chagrined. He reminds me we
had been warned not to swim. And I snap that no one said it
was too dangerous to wade. But we both know we have been
foolish; this is a beach of such isolation that if we had gone
under, we could not have been saved. I am in awe as I work out
the physics of this long wave. We stop now, see its guile, how
it imperceptibly gathers force over rocks and reefs way out,
how it garners ruthless energy, how it would be impossible to
surf or swim or live long in this kind of rush. It is majestic and
hostile and unrelenting and deceptive. The *rough one* is now an
understatement.

This surf, this current, this force: this is what the turtles
swim through.

After the adrenaline has drained out of us, we walk the hard
wet swash, cautiously letting the small waves lap our feet just
enough to keep cool. Now that we know them for what they
are, we are not really attending the waves, but simply watching
where we are in relation to them. What we are really paying
attention to is the high-water line, examining the sand surface
near the scrub edge. Sure enough, only a few hundred yards
down the beach, we come to the first one.

The pattern is beautiful in the damp sand leading from the
water's edge to the scrub thicket, over a hundred feet, a yard
wide and serpentine. The indentations are a script, a topography of will and instinct and necessity, deep and regular corru-
gations with the furrow down the center where the tail drags
as a kind of rudder. It looks like a replica of a complicated
mountain range, one where the hills follow a miniature fault
line of volcanic moraines.

These marks were made by a female.

Sea turtles are made for the water, not the sand. It seems

counter to everything in them except the survival of the species to drag those heavy bodies over the soft sand to a place
where they dig with appendages meant for swimming. They
dig out the sand to a deep bed, then turn and force out dozens of eggs. I have heard they make tears while laying their
eggs. Then each turtle turns, covers the eggs, turns again, and
crawls back, slowly grooving the sand with this instinctive text,
back to Brava, the rough one, and through that hellacious surf.

They do this in the dark.

Each morning, the new nests are marked with stakes, the
orange tape dated the night the nest was made. When the time
comes, scientists, ecologists, nature lovers watch for the hatch,
counting and trying to help the tiny turtles reach the water.
If they make it that far, more of them will live. But until they
hatch, the most important thing is for them to remain undis-
turbed. We stay the designated six feet away from the nests,
look admiringly at the hollow that remains even after the cov-
ering up, at the intricate pattern of tracks, then move to the
next one. We find no new nests to report. All the nests we find
have been staked, but it is early in the season. We visit close to
a dozen nests during the slow hike down the beach. We count
every nest as a blessing on the future. With each one, I am
more and more awed at the mother's journey, at the tenacity
of this internally driven quest through the grip and treachery
of Brava. I better understand Jorge's symbol, the death, the
dance, the dive and resurfacing.

Our last night in Culebra we return to Flamingo Beach. We
have learned much about this island that we have come to appreciate. The wide and lovely beaches, the fish-laden waters,
the constant and generous warmth—not to mention strong
coffee and excellent sun. We have snorkeled every calm day,

for it is the bath that renews the soul, a baptism of regenera-
tion, this swimming on the surface, looking down into the sea.
We have never seen the elongated tear of a bomb still resting on the bottom, or the tears of the great sea turtles, but
we have seen plenty of other industrial shapes—pipes and re-
bar embedded in fractured concrete, parts of tools we cannot
name—enough to convince us that there was another world
here once, and it was not beautiful.

But superimposed over those shadowy shapes, we have
seen the fan and bright flash of coral and its inhabitants. We
have hiked hills and drunk cheap island beer, eaten fresh fish
and conch, and listened in bars late at night to the island mix
of drumming and jazz. We have learned which of the small
makeshift eateries are run by people who know the native way
of food. We have gone back and talked to Jorge, who has told
us more about how the island is inevitably threatened by development and how the locals are becoming demoralized by
the shift in policy that will allow more devastating shoreline
resorts, resorts that will encourage erosion, silt, pesticide run-
off, waste water that could tip the balance for the reefs, fish,
and turtles to a death watch.

He has given us this last set of directions.

It is dusk on Flamingo. Because this is a beach that faces
north, it is the most stunning moment of the day. The sun
drops behind the beach, not on the water, and an even pink
light spreads out. It does not have a source; it is just there, resting on the water and sand. Artist's light. It is quiet at this time
of day; sunset buffs go to the ferry launch where conventional
sunsets dazzle, where there is ice cream and beer. Flamingo is
at its empty best. The low surf rolls lazily, and the spray drawn
off the breaking waves rises and floats, an echo of the wave it
has abandoned.

We walk west toward the sandy point, knowing what we are going to find. I am wondering if this is how I want to mark my last evening on Culebra. We pass the picnic and camping area, where a distant radio plays a fast salsa, and then the last buzz of campers fades away. After a long time, we round the point of the horseshoe, and there it is, visible but still a long way off. Unmistakable. We keep taking the steps that will lead us to this dark shape in the sheer, warm light of the evening, until at last we are standing a dozen feet away.

A historian could tell me what kind it is. I need know only that it is a World War II tank, half-buried in the warm sand, its hatch flipped open and partly blown away so that the rims still reaching up resemble the horned antennae of an enormous iron insect. It is covered with rust and pocked with holes. Its tracks, strange corrugated runs. This is the tank that the military used as a target, this tank, still here fifty years later, at which they aimed and fired and aimed and fired. Sometimes they hit, sometimes they missed, sometimes the shells exploded, sometimes they didn't.

Stay on the paths.

But I also see what Jorge wanted me to see, that this destruction—the way the tank was damaged and then eaten by the salt and years and trade winds—has softened it. It is melting, losing shape, a monstrous blossom gone soft and brown with rot.

And then there is Jorge's symbol.

Painted across the turret, smoothing the surface with bright colors, the emblem of the rising dancer. Jorge's Sea Phoenix, the figure that has been adopted by the activists, young and old, native and transplanted, the symbol of the dancing fish, a creature rising from the dead, diving and dancing and swimming, human and fishlike, painted on the side of a tank so old

and rusted it has ceased to be frightening and is being transformed into something else, a paradox, coming to mean the
opposite of what it once was.

Irony stretches out in the light around us, for the tank and
Jorge's Sea Phoenix are the two protections for this delicate
place. We stare at this artifact of defense and destruction; we
touch it, this mechanical creation maimed by its maker; and
we finally turn away to look again to the forgiving ocean,
watching for the hope that rises from inside the surf, catches a
current, struggles forward hard-shelled with need, to make a
nest out of sand in the amazing night that permeates this small
and fragile paradise.

Squall

Eleven Mile Canyon, Colorado

Sometimes when we live in the day-to-day, in the ordinary, but without being in touch with the sacredness the ordinary should have, we simply drop into the next task and the next, and the days just get longer, and there is no rest, and maybe that's why, when for the first time my sisters—Marijo and Patti—and I gathered at Patti's home in Woodland Park, Colorado, at the end of a grueling winter, Marijo and I fought on the second night we were there. It was all about being way too tired of life and work, and too much wine and too little understanding of things that happened a long time ago, and being apart so long we didn't know each other as well as we thought anymore. It hurt like hell.

It took Eleven Mile to get us straight again.

There are some parts of life that belong to myth. A river
might be one. Eleven Mile is that myth of a river, a place that
should not exist in this world of trouble and work and muck-
ing in the bullshit injustices of the day. It flows out of the
Eleven Mile Reservoir and shoots right past the weight of sadness some of us carry, all the great wildness has left us. Even
after I was there, parts of what happened are unbelievable to
me. Myth, I tell you. A story we made up to save ourselves.

It's cold in Patti's big house built into the side of a canyon
above Woodland Springs. What do we expect? It's a late March
morning. We're in the sunroom, huddled and mostly silent
and for now, not yelling. But when young Ian, Patti's lanky
sixteen-year-old son announces, "If we're gonna go, this is
the day we gotta go," I know I'm in more trouble than I was
the minute before. He looks at the three of us, sister-women
huddled in chairs, a little groggy, more than a little hungover,
staring out at Pike's Peak, thinking *any damn colder than this,
and it will snow.* He says it in the kind of *well this is obvious*
tone that only a sixteen-year-old would dare assume with three
strong-willed, independent women in various stages of meno-
pause. Anyone else would be deferential, or we'd have killed
them, but Ian knows no better, and I for one am too blue to
argue. He and I look at each other, and I think I'm holding a
poker face, that neutral, don't-look-at-me-I'm-not-really-here
face. But the next thing I know, he's hauling waders into the
Explorer, and Patti is brewing another thermos of coffee, and
Marijo is piling up slices of bread just as our mother used to
do when she made sandwich lunches for five back in Michigan,
where we all grew up.

It's only a forty-five minute drive, but I'm nervous as hell
the whole way there. I am the oldest of five and well educated,
some would say accomplished—as my sisters are—but here is

the deal: I am the only one who doesn't know how to fish. The only one. Somehow, back on the Michigan farm where we all learned to walk, when the fishing poles got handed out, I was staring at the sky. When my father took us to the pond to catch chubs and bluegills, I didn't like the mud. When my brothers hauled cane poles to the back creek, I was afraid of the leeches. When my grandpa fished the Hart River behind his house in town, I was picking raspberries.

Both of my sisters grew up to be smart, beautiful women who fish. To add to the injustice, they either married men who loved to fish and who took them fishing, or they raised kids who loved to fish and took them fishing. Or both. And of all the fishing they did, the fishing they love best is fly-fishing. And that's where Ian comes in. I swear, if I'd been smart, I would have taken him out right there.

But then we turn off from the groomed highway, turn toward the rise of mountain split by canyon, where the river lands like a slow wonder after its wild run down the slopes. We drive a long gravel road up the range, past the ranger station and through the river bottom. At that point it stretches out in a plain of openness like something peaceful. It's a cold day, spring-lean with a light coming down on the rocks like a sharp knife. We drive that old road that borders the river and rises with the mountain slopes, and then the gorge narrows, and then the road turns itself into a shelf and hugs the river close-up and personal. Or sometimes the river drops away down some boulder-strewn precipice, where if you look down, your body gets that lurch that reminds you to keep your shit together.

We roll through rock archways still laced with ice, and we dodge potholes the size of small elephants, but Ian knows where he wants to go, and we keep going. We pass a couple

of pickups, a muddy Jeep coming down. One wiry geezer motions us to stop and announces to Patti that there's a hell of a
hatch happening on a pool at the top. But Ian says no, we don't
have the flies for that, and we keep going until we come to a
bend, and he says to his mom, "Right here, Mom," but Patti
already knows. She's pulling to a stop in a worn place just wide
enough for us to be off and for others to pass.

It's a place where the river shallows out, wide and rushy,
and there's some gravel and osier and willow scrub along one
side, and on the other there is a wall of rock that rides up and
back until you can't see. And in the middle is this one big rock,
this monster of a boulder, set right in the river so boldly that
the river has to defer to it, go around it on both sides, and I
see how the river resents that and sluices against it, trying to
wear it away. I see how on one side it's deeper and the water is
darker and faster. And on the near side it's shallower but still
quick, and I wish I knew the names of the water riffles or what
kind of scrub, but I know from looking at the water that if I
were a fish, this would be a good place. There's deadfall and
some river weed, but mostly it's clear tea and fast, and if you
were under that surface, looking up, you could see the fly land,
you could see the sun through that water, it's so clean.

We get out, stand in the wind, hunching against the cold.
Marijo and Ian are discussing flies, and Patti is smiling, her face
to the wind. I'm game and determined to be cheerful, until I
see the costume. The get-up for fly-fishing is like going to the
moon. I've never done this before, so it's something like suit-
ing up for an attack of biochemical bacteria, except there's no
head gear, though there's enough other stuff to make up for it.
To add insult to injury, I am to wear Patti's husband's waders,
and he's a big guy.

Ian swears it will work and I will be comfortable. Marijo and Pat try unsuccessfully not to snicker.

My first step is to pull on the waders, something like rubber coveralls with thick black booties. These come up to my chest and bulge at the groin, and that sets everyone off again. I feel like a giant, well-browned doughboy. Then Marijo gives me the kind of boots that double the size of my feet in all directions. I have trouble bending to lace them and stumble ungracefully against the fender. I try to cover by telling them that I give lessons for this kind of trick on Tuesdays, but then I lose my balance again and sit abruptly on the tailgate, thinking I'll never be able to move. I'll just have to sit here for hours in this rubber armor and try not to feel sorry for myself. They are laughing out loud by now, and don the same get-ups, moving unselfconsciously despite the added clumsiness.

They wait for me; I realize I'm not getting out of this.

Then Marijo turns to me with a big belt in her hands, and I wonder just how mad she was the other night and just what she will really do about it, but she cinches the belt around my chest and says in a calm voice, "If you fall, fall backward, and there will be enough trapped air to keep you afloat for a while."

If I fall? *Oh shit.*

Then we pull up our hoods against the wind, needling sharp, and tuck in our strings. Patti and Ian lumber off through the scrub; mother and son know these waters. But it is Marijo who shows me what to do. It is she who goes first, attaching her rod to her reel forty-five degrees off the top, she who demonstrates how to screw and lock in place the reel to the rod. I follow with my own borrowed rod and reel. She shows me how to run the line through the guides, lets me finger the

line down to the tippet and then to that filament that is like a
strand of hair.

Then like some magician, she dives into one of the many
pockets of her vest and comes up with a small clear box, snaps
it open. In it are bits of flight and sky set in rows, the fuzz of
nature looped to the tiniest of hooks, and she chooses one for
me, and I take this mimicry of buzz—a midge—between my
fingers. I can barely see the tiny metal loop where I will have
to tie the line. She shows me how to run the line through, she
tells me to catch the end and loop it seven times around the
line I am holding taut. She counts with me, and then she tells
me to pull it taut. I lose the line twice before getting it right,
but then I do get it right, and I see my wrap become a small,
glistening knot. She nods and then, *voilà,* snips the excess with
a tiny pair of scissors from yet another pocket. With small pli-
ers, she presses a rough lead weight around a line, its purpose
to sink the line but not too much.

We catch the hooks on the guides, and she lifts the pole
above her arms, and we start through the scrub, walking like
large mechanical bears. She reaches the river first, and as I
come down to the muddy shore, I see that Patti and Ian are
upstream already. I notice how they have set themselves a respectful distance from each other. Is this how it is done, how
we give each other space on a river so that each can carry out
the necessary motions? I see how they are moving slowly, how
they watch each other only peripherally as they move into the
deeper currents. It is a sideways lesson in living.

At the shore I hesitate, but Marijo leads me in, looking back
with a quiet smile, and I step into the river like touching goo
with a toe, expecting to be shocked with cold. Instead I feel
an encompassing pressure, a steady heaviness against my legs
that is not about the cold but about the weight of river, about

the messages of current and flow. I lift my leg to step out further and when I put the boot down into the silty bottom, the boot is drenched with plumes of mud that underwater look like the drift of smoke in wind. Then my boot hits rock, the water clears, and I am steady, if a little tentative. My feet do not feel wet or cold; the black booties are an apparent success. I lift the other foot and this time, at that point where I am balanced on one leg, pulling my other boot nearly through the surface, the current throws me and my boot splashes sideways and I am flailing for balance. I catch myself, but my yelp gets Marijo's attention, and she turns. "Shuffle," she says.

Now we're playing cards? I think I've misheard her.

But she says it again. And then I see how she is moving, how she is not lifting her boots but shuffling her feet along the bottom, feeling forward in a kind of low shamble of steps that do not rise but run parallel to whatever bottom the river is giving. Remarkable. I try the same and feel how it works, how it is the kind of walk that will keep me balanced in the river, that allows we human animals who stand upright, perpendicular to flow, to be in a small way more like the river, the flat gait in our feet at last parallel instead of counter to the river. Marijo and I wade out to a shallow section two feet deep, where the current is swift and the bottom even.

Marijo stares at the rock looming in front of us. I try to see with her eyes. Oh, she is not looking at the rock so much as at the surface of the water—or under it. The river flows through weed beds here and there, but where it divides on our side of the rock, about fifteen or twenty feet away, there is a hollow carved under the rock. "You should try to fish that," she tells me. "You should try to land the fly in that calm spot." I see it, nearly tucked in the rock's shadow, a quieter place along the edge.

I know it is impossible.

Here Marijo pulls her line loose, threading it through her fingers, and shows me how much slack to give, how to pull it free and let it ride on the surface, and then I see that magic, as she shows me her wrist, her arm raising the rod like a wand, and then the clock, where in the arc of the cast, the wrist stops at two o'clock and ten o'clock and then releases. I try the same, imitating clumsily, but how did I not know it would feel wonderful? It is an organic movement, a natural thing, the brain extending into the rod, the sweep of the sky a pleasure. I hear her chuckling. She points out that my eyes were closed and that the cast has landed six feet from the tip of my rod and nowhere near where I aimed.

She suggests, every bone in her body being kind to me, that I just practice for a while.

So I do. I cast off ten or fifteen times. Of those, three land somewhere in the vicinity of the spot where a fish, if it were really hungry, might dart out of shadows and nibble. They aren't hungry. But the cold air is refreshing, the motion is not hard, and the adventure ironic: standing still in a river totally in motion. At some point Marijo leaves me, drifts down beyond the rock. I am not a loner by nature, but I value solitude. And this is a new kind of solitude, a soothing unquiet, serenity full of the unwords of a healthy river, a river that rises and falls with mountain seasons, one that tosses itself down with spring rain and fades with summer drought. It is a river that casts its own spell. I sense all this as I stand alone for the first time in a wild river, practicing a cast I will not master, watching the orange line run out, sometimes farther than I hoped. My cast is always rough, but I begin to understand the release, to feel the way it must loosen. Twice it gets tangled, and I have to stop and do penance for my encounter with a willow tree. Once I come up empty of the midge and have to return to the shore to tie another. The second time I manage the task while standing in the river. Once I feel a vibration in the line, but whatever it is knows I am a rookie and slips away.

Though the wind is cold, my upper body is warm because my arms have taken over the work. The motion becomes a small obsession coursing down to the hands. They want to accomplish this practice of their own accord. The wind scolds more fiercely. Clouds thicken, and high above, the blur of a front rolls across the high ridges. As I reel in the line again— how many times has it been?—the voice of the first snow hisses between the water sounds. The squall slips down the canyon walls and descends like some fierce, wide-winged bird flying over the river. This snow consists of tight crystals only the mountains make, as unlike our softer lake-effect snow as it could be and still be snow. It stings my face and my hands when, yet again, I have to retie. My fingers grow numb, but I lumber back toward the rock, shifting upriver a few dozen feet, then down again, then deeper and shallower, trying different angles, trying to understand the nature of this task, its patience and its craft.

Finally a stiffness rises in my shoulder. I reel in a last cast, break the ritual of repetition, thinking I might try another part of the river. I look around to ask for advice. No one in sight. Because of the snow, I am a little chilled. I suspect I should move out of the wind. I shuffle downriver, around the curve of the boulder for the first time. Here the river broadens, and the current curves, and there is my sister, slipping her line out, one after another, in graceful, long-hearted casts. She is in the river, one knee down and one braced up, and she raises the rod and whips it back and forth so that in the snow and wind, it becomes a shivering darkness, a delicate link between the

current of the squall and the current of the river. Her position
is genuflection, and I see her concentration, her clear eyes, her
hands in their fingerless gloves. She is there, a river goddess
dressed in river garb, running the line through her fingers and
aiming far, far out over the busy waters. Beyond her, farther
down, in a standing pose, Patti is doing the same, and way beyond, there is Ian, the man-boy, casting with the same intense
concentration.

And in this day of bluster and cold where no one will catch
anything, things get clear. This is not about catching fish. Perhaps I romanticize, but I think what this moment is really about
is that filament between sky and strike, the mimicry of insect
all the way to its doom. They are connected, to each other and
to us, and it is about the best thing I could have hoped for on
this first journey into something I cannot do worth shit, but
can care about nonetheless.

I back away, awed and not a little chagrined at this vision
of them, and I let the wind come back to me. I return to my
side of the rock and practice until I am truly cold to my bones.
When my fingers can no longer knock the ice crystals from the
guides, I trundle slowly back to shore, make my way through
scrub to the road. I arrive shivering at the car, and I am startled
to see that they too, by some unspoken, unsignaled agreement
have returned. We climb in, Patti turns on the heat, and we
warm our hands under the blasts of warm air.

I apologize for not having the stamina they seem to have,
but when I finally glance at the clock I gasp. We arrived mid-
morning. It is now midafternoon.

"We can't have been out that long," I sputter, not quite
comprehending where four hours have gone. I really do not
believe we have been here that long and tell Patti something
is wrong with her clock. She laughs at me; Marijo nods know-

ingly. "River time," she says, and when I ask, they shrug.

River time.

We eat sandwiches and drink hot coffee, and they patiently answer my questions, now based on some hard practice. But Ian is not done; he wants more. For him, it is about catching something. And so we drive down a bit, to a place where the river is slower. This time we wade out to the full center, and this time I concentrate my casts on distance more than precision. Marijo and I walk side by side into this muddier section. I try to mimic her whipping motion in the air to get that lovely extension. Again, there comes a time when she drifts away, leaving me to my rough practice. The snow has thinned to an odd ticking, the wind wearing down the hour. I cast a while longer, wading through the thicker weeds, watching their dark, long-fingered writing in the current. Finally Patti taps the horn and I shuffle through these muckier waters, resisting the impulse to lift my boots. The bottom here is less steady, unpredictable despite the shallowness of the river. I step into inches of weed and silt, then onto slippery, underwater rock. One moment I am in up to my thighs, the next balancing on a rock that sets the water at my knees. I'm unsure where to try to climb out. I know I will topple and have to rely on the belt. I will float down to the reservoir. I will slip under and they will tell the story for years.

Standing there in the river, I am suddenly very tired.

Then I see Ian standing where the lip of the shore lowers and a few boot clefts mark the muddy incline. He waves me over. The bank is less rugged here, a handful of small perched steps. I make my way against the current. As I come closer, I can see he is deciding if he should reach out his hand for me or let me struggle up the slippery bank on my own. He finally stands aside, but attentively, and lets me clamber out, and I am actually grateful for this small moment of independence. I know if I am to return to this river, any river, I'll need to figure out how to leave its inner currents on my own—though grace may never be a factor. He has shown me what I needed, a place to come out of the river.

When I get into the car Pat asks where Marijo is.

"I thought she was with you."

But no, they had left her with me. Was she behind or in front? How long has she been gone? No one knows; it's river time we're living. We climb out again, look up and down the river edge, but she is not in sight. Back in, we drive back to the rock. Not there. We turn around and, slowly, watching the currents and the turns, drive down the way we came.

I try not to think about the deep pools, the places where the river gathers itself into a fury through a notch and crashes down in small hard falls. I try not to think how slippery the rocks and bank were when I climbed out, how heavy we all are in our gear. Did she have a belt on? I try not to think of how we fought and how today she helped me with *oh, everything,* teaching me quietly and confidently all the important lessons right down to the secrets.

We three are quiet as we drive slowly, watching for her. Pat says quietly to Ian, "Never ever fish this river alone."

Ian replies without bluster, "She's here somewhere."

But we don't see her. We inch along and come at last to one of the icy arches.

"She couldn't have gotten this far," Ian says, and we back up to a place where the rock bank is so steep we cannot see this side of the river from where we sit in the car, only the rocky darknesses of rushing water on the other side. Its speed scares the shit out of me.

Then.

"I see her rod," Patti says. At first, I understand that means she sees the rod in the water or on the bank and that we have lost Marijo. For a handful of seconds, my heart pounds so hard I know I too will die here on this wild bank of Eleven Mile Canyon.

But no.

What Patti has seen is the tip of Marijo's rod, the top of her cast trembling over the water, shaking its filament down onto this deep and rushing hole. We climb out of the Explorer, and on the edge of the bank, we lean over to see my lovely, strong-willed sister some seventy feet down, straddling boulders, casting like a pro. In that second of relief and discovery, we are given a gift. We see the strike, see the quick jerk, the rise and silver turn of her reel, the hard curve of her rod, and then the glimmering, spotted trout silvering the cold air. We shout and clap, and she turns, grinning quiet triumph as she snares the line. And there she is, lifting her trophy, surrounded by rock and river and cold and success. I tear up from the wind, yell, "Holy shit!" and she nods, not hearing us in the roar of the river but still knowing we have seen her make this single catch of the day, a mythical catch on a river that made us whole again, a river that gave us back to each other, our individual and sisterly collective, a river that cast a rainbow into my sister's hands.

Maps also reflect shifts in our perception of where and who we are and where we are going—that is, shifts in our imagination of the world, our reasons for travel, and what destinations are possible.

James R. Akerman

An American Map

New York City

I. DESTINATION

Because as a child, learning directions—north, south, east, and west—was a great mystery to me, the very idea of a map was like having a paper-folded miracle in a wilderness. Once I understood the *idea* of maps, everything, even my own body, with its *heart on the left side* existed in the possibility of a place. I love the way maps reveal a *here to there* for a person as easily flummoxed as I am. I love the dot-to-dot linear blue, black, red system—our states' highways and towns—the gray squares of platte books—here the Greiner farm, here the Jenson land— and the penciled maps that lead you from my kitchen to your kitchen where the sugar is. Even the map of the voice holds true. I stand in a woods, lost, and if you call my name, you draw a map in my head, and I will come to you.

Three of us—my sister Marijo, her husband, John, and I—follow the map of a heat wave from the upper Midwest to lower Manhattan, arriving at the crest of searing temperatures the last weekend of July. When the cab drops us at a 13th Street brownstone on the lower east side, we step into heat nearly solid in its force. We stand, taking in the not-so-tall older buildings of the East Village, their pocked fronts of brown brick or gray stone, their stoops braced with wrought iron and concrete steps. Squinting, we stare up at the ragged stories of these older apartments as they release heat into the morning. We breathe heavy air. We are in New York City— Marijo and John for the first time, me for the first time in so long that my understanding of where I am on this island has disappeared. Perhaps that is what causes my sense of dislocation.

I am longing for a map.

Our purpose is unique and would be comedic if we weren't so dead serious about it. We are here to promote a documentary film about a vegetable, asparagus, grown in our home fields. Throughout the Great Lakes, but particularly in Oceana County, Michigan, asparagus is the center of a specific economy for a large number of farmers and agricultural businesspeople. Asparagus is my home crop. I grew up in the asparagus fields, and in many ways asparagus *raised up* my siblings and me. It is the crop that kept the farm stable and taught us to work from the age of seven on.

Now, we have come to New York City, where this film, "Asparagus! Stalking the American Life," will premier at the Rural Route Film Festival being held this July weekend. We are representing our family and the asparagus industry to the film industry. John has figured largely in the film's implementation because he has said things that need to be said to lobbyists. He has gone to Washington DC. He has met the Secretary of Agriculture and asked her if there is any good news on the horizon. He, an entomologist by training and a leader by practice, is the director of the National Asparagus Industry Association. He and Marijo, through her work at the Michigan State University Research Farm, have tried to save our corner of the agricultural world. In the tradition of farmers of old, we have come to the market. We intend to keep our dignity, but we are strangers in a strange land, and no one has given us a map.

Imagine us, hauling bags and boxes up the stoop into a tiny lobby, laden with promotional materials and asparagus "product": asparagus salsa, pickled spicy and dilled asparagus, a kind of sauce we call asparagus guacamole. We buzz in. Trudge up four flights. Wrestle luggage down a gloomy hall. Marvel at the multi-lock system on the door. Step into a narrow one-bedroom apartment spanning the length of the building—public rooms to the front, the bath and bedroom to the back, kitchen a central pivot. *Shotgun style,* we'd say—with window air conditioners at each end.

Inside, a haven, cool and dim, dotted with purple and red pillows. Asian prints grace the walls. The overhead lamps light with pull strings dangling like decorated tails. The woodwork has been repainted so many times the cornices have that rounded look that seems almost soft, like candy coating, but the space is comfortably cluttered, the furnishings portable, far from the weighty furniture of our single-dwelling homes. This is where we will stay; like pilgrims, we settle in.

We are greeted by Anne de Mare, a lovely New Yorker with curly brown hair to her shoulders. Her low voice is warm, friendly, full of acceptance. We are disarmed and released from our midwestern self-consciousness. She is one of the filmmakers.

Can a movie tell you who you are in a strange place? Could it locate you in a world? Or must you have a human guide?

I stand at the window and stare down at the street corner where a homeless woman with a scarf over her head and shoulders trundles her packed grocery cart into the shade of an awning. Her hands fall loosely over the handle of the cart. She leans back against the gray stone and looks around as though she is trying to figure out where she is. Which direction is home? Where is the sun, which cannot be seen through the haze and therefore appears to come from every direction?

We have come to New York during a time of international unrest. In the Middle East, the tatters of the Roadmap to Peace are burned in the Israeli/Hezbollah confrontation. The Iraq war grinds on, ladening the national psyche with a weighty ambivalence. Though our story of a little-known crop grown in a less-known county in distant Michigan may be a microcosm of what is happening to farm-based cultures throughout the world, little hope exists that the issues the film explores—American trade and misapplied drug treaties—will be resolved, no matter how well done the film. There seems even less hope that the long-term stability of our nation can be touched by art or storymaking. Still, we come here in the hope that by showing a film, greeting people, and answering questions, by being generous and by telling a good story, change could lift its head and open possibility. Farmers come to town.

II. HADES AND STARS

Cartographically, strict adherence to the geography above ground is not essential to wayfinding below.

Today, Friday, Anne proposes a brief tourist adventure before we go to the Anthology Film Archives theater, where Anne and Kirsten will pass out flyers and invite people to the film on Saturday.

We descend into the subway, buy tokens, stand in the cellar-air of the lower city. Because we live so much of our lives in open air, it is a claustrophobic, threatening experience. The trains drown speech, and we hold thought in place, pausing midsentence until the discord that is a train passes. We join uncountable bodies sluicing into the air-conditioned cars. We stand, hanging on to poles, learning to sway. I stare at the sub-way map, the elongated lineation of the underground. In this map, it does not matter what the distance is or what the terrain looks like. There is no terrain. The terrain is the train and the people on it. People step on, or scurry off. We watch them, reading them like signs written in an unfamiliar language. Marijo whispers, asking why no one will meet our eyes. I have more experience with this gesture toward anonymity than she does. I know that it can be anything from the simple need for privacy where privacy is at a premium to serious self-protec-tion that keeps us from eye contact. But I understand the im-pulse of her question. We miss the simple warmth of our mid-western interactions, which, even if superficial, still remind us of who and where we are. We believe eye contact can locate a person in the world as solidly as a road map. Maybe the ques-tion isn't so much where we are as we move under this city, but who we are.

Grand Central Station is an architectural phenomenon with a skymap. Its interior heights make people seem like bugs hur-rying through a glimmering cave. The high arc of the ceiling, its blue and gold universe, catches and sweeps our attention to its constellations, which are, Anne tells us wryly, backward. By some design error, the celestial universe was applied in reverse on this majestic ceiling. I think of how our beloved North Star would mark something entirely opposite in an upended hemisphere, how the Big Dipper would dip the wrong way. Would we become even more thoroughly lost under these inverted constellations? Would the stories they represent also turn on their heads? Would Orion's belt and quiver turn into tools of peace? Or would we get used to this, let our experience of it become the way we saw the world?

Marijo wonders how one can pass through a space such as this and not look up. We feel small and awed, but now and then a passerby sees our awe and smiles and we do meet her eyes. We are overly delighted when this happens, grateful to people who have seen us and do not seem offended at our plain wonder, seem in fact proud of this place, this turned-about center of their universe. Still, they move as though they know where they are going. We move as though we do not.

Anne leads us to the Campbell Apartment, a dark-beamed bar with an inlaid ceiling, which is actually tucked into the station, where table attendants wear black cocktail dresses and white pearls. The single sensational room and elegant open loft were an apartment home for a wealthy man. It feels more like a church and choir to us, but we willingly pay $12.00 a glass for a delicious Zinfandel and settle into deep chairs in front of a huge but empty fireplace. I slip off my shoes and tuck my feet under and am immediately asked by one of the bepearled women to put my shoes back on. *Toto, we are not in Kansas anymore,* I think to myself. Marijo asks what kind of beams traverse the ceiling. No one knows, and she finds this amazing, that one could live and work in a place graced by such well-crafted beauty and not know the wood that makes it beautiful. Still we appreciate the room's impulse, a spacious privacy in the midst of a crowded anonymity. A place within a place, an oasis of scale after coming out from under the earth and through the backward constellations of the station. A byway. A stopping place on the pilgrimage.

Sitting there in that elegant tourist spot, John and Anne speak of the finances for the film—ever precarious. We talk about Anne's life as a native New Yorker, a successful playwright and independent filmmaker, her surprise to find herself working on a documentary that takes place in a small community halfway across the country. When Anne slips away to make a call, Marijo tells me that Anne has a *country heart,* and I believe it, for she is as down to earth and warm as one could wish. But on reflection, I can't help but notice how we are surprised by this—we have believed the stories brought back by other travelers.

Why wouldn't we expect to find warm and generous people in this city?

Why are we so suspicious?

My internal map shifts, my perceptions slide over to make room for this new awareness.

When she returns, Anne tells us we should walk back to the bar on 13th Street, where we will meet more people involved in the project. A storm is due to blow through the city, and preliminary breezes will stir and lift the heat—it will be cooler now on the streets. Marijo and I are delighted—though we could not say which pleases us more: that Anne is reporting the weather or that the prediction allows us to walk outside, in real air.

Out on the streets, immense billboards pock the city canyons, flashing on and off like gargantuan fireflies. I am so distracted that I fall behind and have to reorient myself to where my people are. Once I stop, staring at a window with forty

TVs. When I turn away, I am lost again.

New York is an orderly city, the numbered streets, alphabet-ical avenues announce where you are. It is as steady as the back forty field, once you know the landmarks. But I can't remem-ber how the numbers coordinate with the cardinal points. Are lower numbers east or west, north or south? We are following street numbers *downtown* but I keep trying to figure out where I am in relation to rivers, the ocean, or people. Young dread-locked men in cutoffs run in the heat; spike-haired women in strappy blouses briskly pull carry-alls of groceries; young cou-ples wheel strollers over curbs with an efficiency that barely disturbs their children. Most seem to be forty or under, many in the twenty-something range. How did they get here? I pass several homeless people and wonder too—how did they get here? What is their story, their map? I don't romanticize their situations, but I wonder if they are merely lost differently than I am? Or do they know their interior maps far better than I know my own?

Do they know where to go?

How long do we follow Anne's knowledgeable stride through masses of people and horn-punctuated traffic? She is a New Yorker who, by glancing briefly at those corner num-bers, knows where she is and how far she must go. We finally round a last corner on to 13th Street, into view of the red neon glimmer of the Detour Bar. We climb a concrete step into the coolness. Before we clear the threshold, we are hailed by Evan, the friendly bartender. His voice anchors me at last in a place. I have always loved local bars—they are center to many stories. We belly up, and when I slip off my shoes, no one scolds. The wine is half the price it was at the Campbell, and it's happy hour.

Evan has agreed to sponsor the post-film reception the next

day. Anne is discussing the final details for the party. Asparagus
martinis, extra asparagus-based snacks, chips and crackers for
a small army. Wine. A lot of wine. The shoebox-style room
seats no more than forty people. Will it be enough room? We
are looking around, getting a feel for the black jazz tables and
funky vinyl chairs when Kirsten Kelly, the other filmmaker, arrives breathless and bubbling. Kirsten is the midwestern connection to the Big Apple. She grew up on an asparagus farm in
Shelby, Michigan, in the same county we are from, before she
was accepted to Juilliard and came to the city to study theater
and filmmaking. Her father was a farmer who, as the asparagus industry and agriculture itself changed, decided to sell.
She still misses it, and it is her concept that initiated this film.
She is dark-haired, bright-eyed, and has the kind of full smile
that flits and then stays. As she and Anne stand together, exchanging details, the dedication from both is clear and seems
longstanding. Marijo and John order a round of much less expensive wine, and we all strategize about the next day. The
film will show at 1:00 on Saturday, not the best time of the
day—too early—and we need to encourage a crowd. We decide to attend the festival tonight, not to see the films but to
mingle and schmooze and get out the word.

III. WAYFINDING

Wayfinding maps, it seems, do not just tell us
where we are going, but also tell us who we are.

The entrance of the Anthology Film Archives building, a
three-story red brick, is marked by an arch inlaid with detailed
fox and hounds in red stone. Past that nod to a grander past, its
character is functionality to a fault—belying the good work it

does. The ticket office is unadorned and boxy, the floor clean but worn, the ceilings plain. The welcome table is laden with Rural Route Film Festival T-shirts—Allis Chalmers orange with a tractor design—and brochures on tonight's films. We meet the young directors of the festival as well as volunteers, participants, friends—all characterized by an earnestness that surprises me. For the festival, they have selected films that reveal a deep respect for the rural world, small farms, and independent food producers. How did these people end up in New York? They do not look lost.

What pilgrims these?

We unwrap and open jars of asparagus guacamole and salsa. We pour it out into pretty ceramic bowls, set it onto bright plates, and surround it with chips. Then we carry them to the lobby. *Would you like an asparagus movie appetizer?* Here in New York City, with perfectly straight faces, we talk "crop." Marijo speaks to people about the plant's life cycle and harvest. John answers questions about the agricultural industry. Kirsten and Anne speak of being literally "in the fields" making the film. Because it is the only thing I know how to do with any authenticity, I encourage people to eat. I talk about the flavors of asparagus, the spices that go with it, the way you can prepare it. *And won't you try this asparagus guacamole?* I ask a red-haired woman wearing glittering cat glasses. She does, and she comes back for seconds.

We invite everyone, from film buffs to people on the street to the viewing on Saturday. When the last film funnels the crowds out of the lobby and into the theater, we seal the jars, pack away the green T-shirts that proclaim, "I Love Michigan Asparagus." The sales pay for the entry fees for still more film festivals. Anne and Kirsten's film has garnered good reviews at the Full Frame Festival in North Carolina and the Saugatuck

Festival in Michigan. This is how the independent film market-
ing works.

But this is New York City. We are all nervous about Saturday. Have we touched enough people?

Then we are out on the streets again, and I am again trying to figure out where we are. Cars, cabs, buses, bikes, even
horses, roar and squeak and wheeze and clomp past us. Despite the breeze, the temperature has not dropped. It is 10:00,
and we are ravenous and—how can this be—restaurants are
still open at this time of night. Not just restaurants but shops,
markets, pharmacies. We laugh as we straggle along, window
shopping, oohing over the tumble of tulips and exotic flowers
lining the sidewalks in buckets.

In any of our small towns of Hart or Shelby or Crystal Valley, stores close at 5:30, restaurant grills at 9:00, bars by midnight, even on a weekend. And though we know any number
of homes where we could show up at midnight and someone
in an old-fashioned terry cloth robe would fry us an egg-and-
mayo sandwich, we are delighted with the array of late-night
dinner options. We snaggle through late crowds, finally settling into an open-air Italian restaurant called Paprika, where
everyone orders the fettuccini with grapes, shrimp, and of
course, asparagus. We are exhausted from heat and crowds,
from talking and the sense of being un-home. But we can still
eat. Our farmer people understood that this is how one rests.

We have become progressively aware of how Anne and
Kirsten are multi-tasking, taking care of us and every other
responsibility to make the film successful. Both are dedicated
to theater, film, and the world of making stories, but filmmaking is neither woman's day job. Kirsten is a freelance director;
Anne, a purveyor of maps—someone who helps collectors
find and buy old maps. In her case, the maps are historical.

Both Marijo and I are interested in this, but we don't know exactly what it means, so our questions are general, imprecise.

Saturday morning launches with a quick tour of a New York City farmer's market. If we are going to find it, this is where. We touch the fresh tomatoes, peppers, zucchini—their season is close to ours—flowers and preserves and more. Here are artists and yarn makers—Marijo buys a half pound of raw wool for Christmas crafts. Sadly, the one vegetable we came for, late-season asparagus, is nowhere to be found. We face the fact that the asparagus—for we have decided to serve two dishes at the premier that call for fresh chilled asparagus—will have to be imported. The asparagus will have been shipped via our primary international competitor, Peru. We all feel the hypocrisy in this, but there is little we can do about it. To help people understand the issues, they must literally taste the threat. We hope the asparagus muses (and our own farmers) will forgive us.

Asparagus rollups are simple as sunshine. Working in an assembly line system in Kirsten's tiny but cheerful kitchen, we spread a slice of ham or turkey with whipped cream cheese and roll it around a stalk of steamed and chilled asparagus. Some recipes call for dill or basil, but we keep this simple, wanting the flavor of the asparagus to carry the day. We make about ten dozen. Then in a flurry, we pull on green T-shirts, pack up more chips and asparagus salsa. In my arms I carry the large platter of fresh asparagus out the door, down four flights and out on to the street, where this time we hail a cab. We pass a homeless man who hears us talking about asparagus. He announces, "Hey, I like asparagus a lot." I stop, lift the cellophane and hand two stalks to him. He accepts, but adds that he'd "really like it with butter."

Of course, who wouldn't want it with butter?

We find the Anthology Film Archives building locked. Here is our spiritual pilgrimage for the day, and we are approaching the holy shrine, but the doors are locked. Then, as we wait, Mrs. Asparagus 1987 arrives in a cab, climbs out in a white gown and satin sash, her tiara shimmering. She is the most faithful of the Asparagus queens, all married women with families who give up a year to travel in support of the green stalk. Some continue, as she has, to give volunteer time long after the moment the crown is handed off. She and her husband flew from Michigan just to meet and speak with "folks."

Volunteers in orange Rural Route tees join us, then filmgoers on bikes, in walking shoes, in cabs—all gather to purchase tickets. Not to miss any opportunity, we introduce ourselves, pass bottled water, speak of asparagus, tell people if they come back, they can taste *real asparagus rollups*. From Oceana County. In Michigan.

Oh. (long pause) *Are they good?*

You'll love them.

They take us in stride.

Finally, heavy doors swing open, and we sweep into the now-familiar lobby. We uncover platters, unwrap rollups, and begin to promote this documentary about the world of the farmer and our agribusiness. The crowd, some 100-plus people in the small theater, is mostly young. A man in a yarmulke tastes the salsa tentatively, a girl with a baby in a sling tries the rollups, twin boys with curly Afros open their mouths, bite down, chew, at first cautious and uncertain, then surprised and pleased. They return again and again for the stalk and dip. We smile and nod as good midwesterners do at a feed. *Have some more, there's plenty,* I hear my mother's voice from across the miles. *And take seconds.* And many do, standing around waiting for the film to begin. We share food, the best ambassador. They laugh, warm to us and to the idea of this strange vegetable meaning something in the world. Even if they came here on a hot Saturday afternoon because these tickets were cheaper than the multiplex, they like the surprise of this vegetable in their festival, the idea that this crop must be saved, that this film is a *resistance,* is *doing something.* I begin to see how these numbered streets, the tiny apartments might be linked to real farms.

Lights flicker. The audience, wiping fingers on green napkins, quiets as they drift up the next level into the darkness of a box-like theater. Before we follow into the cool, we do what good country women do: we consolidate platters, snap on lids, layer it all into coolers, and shove everything out of sight. Then we climb the stairs to the upper theater. I have seen a number of the film's cuts, but not the final version. Marijo and I slip into seats toward the back, so we can leave quickly to get back to the food. The festival director walks onto the screen stage in his festival uniform, jeans and the orange shirt with its white tractor. He is as natural and unpretentious as anyone in authority could possibly be as he offers information points and makes introductions. Marijo and I settle back, a little tired from all that talking, waiting for him to introduce the film.

Surprise in New York City is perhaps sweeter than anywhere because you never expect to be singled out, never assume you will be recognized for anything in light of all the other momentous things going on at any one time.

Or is that another midwestern misperception?

The director stops, clears his throat. It is the quiet change in stance that alerts us. Then he warmly announces that "Asparagus! Stalking the American Life" has been awarded *best*

film of the festival. I can't see Anne and Kirsten up front, but I
see John's head lift and turn in surprise. This calm man who
seldom betrays his feelings is startled momentarily out of his
steadiness. My sister looks at me, laughs, and we high-five in
the dark.

Then the director talks about how skillfully the story unfolds, how the judges thought it captured a sense of hope, despite the failures of policy and legislation. Then he awards the
directors a backpack. We and the rest of the audience laugh.
Still, little raises consciousness like recognition. The faces of
this lively crowd become more attentive; they begin to learn
even before it begins. The room darkens. I watch with the
same attention, renewed by the consciousness that something
has gone terribly right.

On the high screen in New York City, I watch the asparagus
fields of my home. I watch farmer after farmer bend to the
dirt, lift bushels, drive tractors, check bug damage, answer cell
phones and lift more bushels. Here, so far away but right here,
are the faces of my family, their strong bodies working the
long rows of a thirty-acre asparagus field, *breaking the spear.*
I see my brother Tom run his hand through pallets of green
stalks, hear his authority as he arranges for weighing in, load-
ing semis, hauling itineraries. I watch migrant workers bend
to the dirt from the mechanical riders. I listen to farmers with
family names so familiar they are the litany of our childhood.

Marijo and I watch our brothers' faces on the screen, inter-
viewed in the cabs of their pickups, in barns, on forklifts, and
in the fields. In one scene John explains what happens when
we are ignorant of the repercussions of global trade. He tells
why tariffs were removed from Peruvian asparagus—to offer
an alternative to the cocaine agriculture—but in the process
our own farmers were sacrificed. In another scene, my brother

asks how he can compete with Peruvian asparagus if the Peruvian farmers don't have to pay their workers more than two dollars an hour. I'm proud when he announces, captured on film as he stands in his Carhartts at his cooling machine, that he would *pay workers twenty dollars an hour,* but he wants a *level playing field* with his competitors.

The film details how the tariffs were lifted on imported asparagus in order to dissuade Peruvian farmers from succumbing to the drug trade, and how the United States actually helped start the asparagus industry in Peru. But it goes on to explain that the farmers grow cocaine in the mountains. Asparagus is grown in low elevations, in the desert flatlands. And though the film is quick to point out that the amount of cocaine smuggled out of Peru is now less, the amount in neighboring Bolivia has increased dramatically. The audience is quiet except for an *oh* of understanding when a scene shows asparagus growing on the irrigated desert in Peru.

I watch the faces of old friends come and go as the film unfolds the story of our National Asparagus Festival, of our queen's title, Mrs. Asparagus, a woman chosen because she is mature and already plays a knowledgeable role in the farm. How practical not to choose a young ingenue. I watch the men who build the queen's float talk about *never losing a queen,* and a shout of laughter goes up from this New York crowd. I listen to John speak of the legendary aphrodisiac properties of asparagus, while Marijo's wide onscreen smile brings a giggle of delight to the audience. We see the final scenes of harvest at night, under threat of storm, and I remember nights like those, racing to finish a picking.

After the standing ovation, after the second introduction of the directors to more enthusiastic applause, the most pressing question is: "What can we do?" And so John and Marijo, Anne and Kirsten and Mrs. Asparagus 1987 fill them in on purchase patterns, letters to congress, workable trade agreements, and more practically, which fresh produce supports both the farmer and the purchaser. They speak of things as simple as asking a grocer where a crop, not only asparagus but any crop, comes from, and how to insist on country of origin. We realize this is an audience of doers. We become elated as, at the end, they applaud long and hard, appreciation riding on the sound. I am amazed at how this audience listens, at how eager they are to know, at how they seem to understand what farms mean. Though this is only a microscopic slice of the city's population, they are invested. Another preconception falls to dust.

I break out the champagne. For me, the film was even more than the much deserved and important success for Kirsten and Anne. It was at last recognition for John and Marijo, for their amazing role in keeping the fields alive.

All that afternoon, we toast the green stalk that has brought us to the city. We toast the success of the film that tells its story. People meet our eyes and we meet theirs. We are not so naive as to think the world has changed, but we float on the pleasure of warm handshakes, the eagerness to sign up for the mailing list, the repetition of the words *Keep us posted*. An older woman reaches up, pats John's face, says, "Good man." After yet another toast to the directors, we scurry out, for the there is a party to be had at the Detour Bar.

When, late at night, after asparagus martinis at the Detour, we come out onto the warm street, and for the first time I turn in the right direction toward the 13th Street walk-up, I feel less lost, as though their authentic concern gave us a way to know where we were in this city. A map of connection, a way into our hearts.

IV. FROM HERE TO THERE

> But dedicated travelers know that finding our way through
> the world is as much a journey of the spirit, a means of
> identifying our personal and cultural identities, as it is a
> navigational challenge.

Then we are given Sunday, a free day in the Big Apple. Buzzed
on coffee, exhaustion, and exhilaration, and a little hungover, we follow Anne through Central Park. We wander, a
little awed at this constructed green space among skyscrapers.
Marijo is delighted with the sculpture of the *Alice in Wonder-
land* mushroom with its formidable caterpillar; I am thrilled at
seeing the winged angel from Kushner's *Angels in America*. We
encounter plants we cannot name and trees we do not know.
We pay a man a dollar to look through a telescope at the red-
tailed hawks high on a building across the park. We think this
a strange thing to do in the middle of a huge city, to pay to
look at birds that fly freely over our fields, but we are glad for
the hawks.

Then Anne offers a remarkable thing, to take us to her place
of work, an older building near the United Nations Plaza. "A
bit of a walk, but would you like to see some maps?" she asks.
Of course. Past the flags of the Plaza, past the old church,
through a building with Rivera murals, up an older-style eleva-
tor, into a warren of small offices.

First, the globes, so large that I see them as furniture, stately
and shapely. Here are two, a matched pair set in twin cradles
so that each turns freely, without axis. One I recognize, the
blueprint of earth from the stars' point of view, staring down
at a wayward but beloved sphere. But the other is like the sky
ceiling in Grand Central Station, only righted. Anne stands,

her fingertips touching each cradle. She tells me, "Like lovers, globes come in pairs, earth and sky."

Oh, one globe is a map of the world, the other a sphere of our stars. Designed to be used together at a time when travelers attended the sky as much as they did the land, one informs the other. I think of a time when knowing the sky kept us from being lost, and now we know so little of the sky because we cannot see it. I have never seen them paired like this, connected so that we see first from the point of view of sun, and then from even further out, from . . . God's view, tracking where we are by stars that, in distance, become as small as our daily losses.

Anne leads us on to a row of atlases with beautiful hand-painted maps of this country and of Europe. She tells us stories of her boss combing European countries to discover American maps. That's where our most important maps come from because "There was great interest in the new world," she says.

The new world.

I watch her looking at us over the wide dark table at the center of the office, and I think she is assessing us. This woman has led us intrepidly over the city, and we have followed, trusting her leadership and her knowledge. Her face shifts, and she makes a small decision. She turns to a wall graced with a map of the lower east side at the turn of the nineteenth century. There is a safe. She tumbles the locks by memory, swings open a heavy door and reaches in. With both hands, she takes out a flat box and brings it to the table. She is careful as she opens it. She lifts a thick folded sheaf, about ten by six. She places it on the center of the table. The map is backed by treated muslin or linen. Though we can tell it has seen hard use in its time, it is still sturdy, the high quality paper and cloth still holding together an older world. With great care, she begins to unfold it, first the long way, so it looks like a runner on the table, and then the other way, like wings. She is vigilant and slow as she does this work. When it is fully unfolded, she looks at it kindly, as though it were a beloved child lifting its face.

It takes a while to recognize.

Open before us, as they were conceived and understood in the late 1700s, a portion of the thirteen, without the boundaries of state. The map is centered on Virginia, dense with detail, hand-drawn and colored in blues and greens, but also it reveals a wide slice of what became the original eastern colonies. Here are territories so old—Louisa, Amelia, Isle of Weight County—they have no formal boundaries. The names are placed over a region, and nothing designates the beginning of one or the ending of another except the rivers. The rivers, inlets, harbors, and coastal plains are most carefully delineated and crowd the space with their wiggles and turns. The regions to the west are bordered by a wrinkled white space, a vast tract by which we might infer emptiness. This would become us, the Midwest.

We look at Anne.

"We bought it in France. We knew what it was, and that it was old and probably colonial. But not its significance."

We wait, not sure what she is telling us. The name, when it comes, seems too soft, does not at first ring with any familiar images.

"Lafayette's," she nods.

I ransack my U.S. history.

She continues, "He used many maps, but this is probably one he used to help George win the Revolution. It was drawn by Robert Fry and Peter Jefferson."

I don't remember who Robert Fry is but Peter Jefferson . . . *Thomas Jefferson's father?*

I take a long slow breath as it comes back. Lafayette was the French captain who wintered with Washington at Valley Forge, who paralyzed Cornwallis at Yorktown until reinforcements came. Without Lafayette's campaign with Washington, the first settlers and would-be citizens would have lost the country. Through him, the war was essentially won. Despite its lack of boundaries, his map offered him enough sense of location, of where he was placed on this barely charted continent that he could then make the decisions that would, for good or ill, help establish this country. His map rests on the table before me. We are quiet, losing ourselves in the pale greens and blues, in the borders that are no longer borders, in the ones that are.

Here is a map of our beginnings as a nation.

Our country's spirit map: For those precarious and ill-defined spaces housed the great will and ambitious freedom and honest need and blind opportunity whose effects domino through time, perhaps along the way tumbling the factual history of who we are as Americans and leaving in its place the complex, multi-dimensional narratives that still influence us. Those time-born and time-worn routes lead all the way to our own struggles fighting for a farmer's way of life gone astray in a global economy. This is the map that showed Lafayette, the young and brilliant commander, where he was in this new country, how to get from here to there. All weekend, moving through this city that is the pulse of America, I have tried to feel less lost, I have longed for a map. I have tried to understand *from here to there*. I wonder what it means to come here to promote a movie about a vegetable nearly comic in both shape and value, and yet so valued by people of character, like the people who would have picked up arms for the conqueror-soldier Lafayette.

Is this the map I asked for?

This is the one I am given, one that carries with it immense history that for a moment not only connects me as farmer to city, but connects me in time, as current citizen to my country's past. Here is the dream map, and like a dream, it is only partially charted, simultaneously prescient and ignorant of the territories and futures it reveals, what its white space conceals. I am aware of the complexity and ambivalence and sometimes malevolence this map infers—for it is journey through time as well as space. And in that time, the psyche of my country evolves.

Here, spread before me, its blocks of colors marking borders we pushed and expanded, crossed and recrossed, trying to find another place, to be somewhere else, to grow food or build homes, cities, then states. Justly or not, we have come from other places and mapped a land not always ours to map, the map itself becoming both understanding and claim. Even among practical farmers, the drive to make the land our own, to shape it into "value," something that feeds the body and ambition, may be thrilling and addictive. But I suspect the drive also stems from a need to perceive ourselves as the starting point of a process that will continue, as Lafayette and Washington may have hoped. It is to place ourselves not only where the maps of our nation began, but to place ourselves on a continuous map of self-perception, one that moves in me still, from field to cinema, from street corner to globe, from the map of the ironic backwards sky in Grand Central Station to the moon and what it means. I am here, in this New York, staring at the colorful yet still incomplete beginnings of that continuum. I reach out and with my fingertip I touch its old linen tenderly. I am of it and in it, and I am one of the places marked. May this map of the spirit lead me, lead all of us, in the right way.

The River Inside (A Prose Poem)

Huzzah River, Missouri

Listen, how could I know we would end our stay there with a visit to a cemetery, with the trip to those living graves and a church house on a hillside overlooking the Huzzah River that had just run sorrow through valleys and plains, flooding all the way to the Mississippi?

But I am ahead of myself.

Before all that, there was Easter week, and the cool, new-green days of early spring. Before that, there was settling on the porch of the hundred-year-old house with beers and wine and catching up and admiring the horses and the one donkey who brays once a day, and there was looking over the rough compound of barns and pumphouse and henhouse and feed-house and two other cabins where my David's family live when they live here on the river, which is every chance they can get—though St. Louis is where their work is. Despite that, the life they have made on this five hundred acres, on the rise and plain of just-flooded river, is the one they like better.

How were we to know what a river would be like after a Holy Week flood, that it would still toss with opaque water, shouting its anger in the headlong rush of moving aside the world, its willful need to push itself out of itself. In its wake, all is off kilter: buildings dip and sour their foundations, fences become tangled walls of oak leaf and plastic and tires and lost tackle. An empty picture frame catches in a branch eight feet up, and the current runs through the frame for hours. Everything leans the way of the flood, for to lean against it is to lose footing and be swept away to a stranger place still.

We come from Michigan just after the height of this temper, and we stay through the falling-down time, when each day the level drops and the land rises through the mud, a brown and tree-pocked leaning, a gray-headed turtle revealed but not yet awake. This is the land we walk with Carolina Moon (Caroline for real, Moonie for short) and her adult son Justin, and other of David's beloved cousins, mine, too, by association and spirit. This is the land we traipse, gathering mud like sleeves over our shoes, down to the low, newly washed and roughed banks to search, with the children, Jake and Maddy, for the bird point arrowheads. And after that hour, having turned up only chips of the infamous Missouri flint, these are the fields we squelch through to the heron rookery to sneak up on their high and ill-formed nests.

Though we spot them through the soaring sycamore and hear the croak and bark that warns their world is not well, they spook and fly, chortling into air, and we are given only glimpses of gangly shape, spiky beaks, their ragged lift and circling, never enough for me, never enough of watching wings, hearing some feather-bound voice catch on the wind. We turn away, leave them to their leggy treetop perches. And at the next creek, Justin bends to the bank and from the mix of stone and pebble, lifts a near perfect bird point from the muck.

This is the place where after a day of walking, we are invited to Justin's cabin, where, inside, he has built a tank for river fish. Oh, not just any tank, but one so large it has a foundation and rises as an architectural moment in his living room, four by four by ten feet, with filtered watered the color of the river once it clears, that cooled tea. Here are fourteen rivery ones, bass and sunfish, goggle eye and cat fish, and five lovely turtles, one snapper who will get to stay only so long as he doesn't eat one of the fourteen. Once he eats his first, Justin takes him back to the river. The painted is my favorite, his sweet patterns carved with a touch of river weed. Oh, and yes, the weeds. Justin has them all in his tank, and so has replicated the river inside his house.

I ask him why he brings them in, thinking he must be studying them, thinking that to duplicate a river habitat inside your house must mean you want to understand the cycles and behaviors, the ways of the creatures—but no. Justin's warm voice, a single-pitched drawl, tells me he brings them in because he likes them. Yes, he *learns about them and all that,* but he likes to watch them, to have them near, to watch the drift of fish, the slow flip of fin, the whisker of the catfish brushing the bottom stones. If he owns a TV, we don't see it. On a platform overlooking the tank is the full body of a pure white taxidermy deer, its pink glass eyes glittering. I can almost hear its voice, but not just yet.

There is one day, at Justin's direction, we follow a tributary of the Huzzah, Lost Creek, named for an incident when someone, an uncle?—no one can remember who it was exactly—got lost following it. Imagine, getting lost following a river. We cross and wade the shallows to a place where we can sit and think a long time. There again, in the thinking, almost, almost another voice.

And on the way back, we find them, Justin and the children, "excavating" the site of a house that burned perhaps as far back as the Depression, and they invite us to join in archeological digging, uncovering a *secret secret past* (Maddy tells me) on a high hillside overlooking the Lost. Red Cedar and Honey Locust saplings sprout gangly in what would have been a home, but we can find the soft outlines; then Justin stumbles on a threshold of stone. And David and I catch their adventure in dirt, lift the spoons and pry gently for the artifacts of a time that to us is not so long ago, but to the children is as good as dinosaurs.

And that is the first time, in old Missouri, the state that is a border state in more ways than one, that they gather for me, there in the dappled light, those people of the past. I see them only in the parts we find, their rough hands on the drawer-pulls and pottery, now shards. His hand lifts the hook latch, hers shelve the blue Mason jar now melted to an ill-formed amulet. There, cutlery half eaten through with rust cuts the raw loaf, and hinges from a window that must have opened over the stove. Is that where the fire started? I hear her sigh, her Missouri voice, *It always starts with the stove, you know?*

Below the site, I find a patch of chives and violets just starting up—yes, there was a woman.

Later, I hold a brown snake in my hands—a loan from Jake, who is collecting. It turns and coils in my palm and I let it rest in warmth for a while before returning it to the territory of his childhood.

I do not hear them again until the last day. Easter. Or the day after. Warm and river calm at last. We lift our bodies from ham sandwiches at the red harvest table and walk over the low bridge, across the field where beef cows settle on new grass, to the Sellers place, to meet Jerry and Sandra, both soft-voiced women, poetry in their lilt, and Gilbert, just recovering from the lung surgery that *set him back a spell* this winter. They seem glad to see their neighbors and are friendly to us strangers because of it. He is the elder, Gilbert Sellers. He walks slow, but will see us out to the east by south hillside over the Huzzah. "Prettiest stretch of the Huzzah," says Carolina Moon. He nods the old way, all that needs to be said, and he knows it. He unlocks the chain, throws the clasp on the steel gate, and we walk in.

Here are all the old ones of his family, and the ones from another time. Here are the ones who died too young, the infants who never found their way to this light, old ones who were ready for that other light, middling ones who may have had any one of a thousand stories. They rest next to the church house, next to the tin-roofed open-air patio with the long trestle table, where the Memorial Day potluck is still held each May.

There are those who would fault me for skipping the dates of their lives, but it is the names I covet, those I want to touch and know.

They are generous.

First are his people, Ira and Alpha Sellers, good names to descend from, then Lourdeen E. Sellers, Rita Faye Nettles Sellers, and, as if we had said the names out loud, I see them, a generation apart, setting the table under the awning. They are joined by Woodrow Tinker, and a slew of other Tinkers rise up off the hill and lumber down and join us. When I notice

David Lee Tinker was a soldier and died in sixty-seven, I ask if
it was Vietnam that took him, but Gilbert lays his hand on the
stone, and shakes his head, disgust in the line of his mouth.
"No," he says, "Those boys was bad, both of 'em died young
and rough. Hung out with the wrong folks, ran into trouble."

I hear those boys whooping in the distance, hear the rifle
cock and the glass shatter down the pretty stretch. I turn to
Finnis Turnbough who is paying no mind to the youngsters
but calling on some of the others. *Company is here so mind yur
manners.* So Phoeba rises, her skirts laughing in the wind, and
then Wilma and Huron, and friend Granvel Peak, the one who
got stuck under the tractor, and didn't he just know *horses were
better.* He is up on the ridge near Pearl Maud Payne, whose
name is like her life if we could know the inside of anyone
by her name. Odine and Willard Eaton come next, still flirting with each other, and because they are happy to be awake
today, they rouse up Sidney and Francis Hickman, and then we
are back to the Tinkers, Woodrow, and the Turnboughs, old
Noah E. There is Marcus Lane and Radius, pronounced *Radus,*
Gilbert tells us, and Radius chuckles and rubs the stubble on
his chin, and spits tobaccy just shy of Dora Watson's cane. She
humphs and says to Hershel Laird that she never had much use
for Tinkers anyway.

Gilbert lays his hand on one rough stone and says, softly
"This here boy . . ." but then Freadia Blanche Laird's name is
called out by our own Jake, young and alive, reading the hand-
carved letters, and we think she is the oldest, and whatever the
trouble was in Gilbert's tale gets lost as she starts up the gossip
'round about Venita Dahle, who was a kind of doll to all the
men, and pretty Ellen Wisdom who was maybe not at all what
her name claimed. Then comes striding Lena Turnbough,
whose good principles straighten them all out. She calls to the

Hogans, Penelope Anne and her son Harry Lee, who escaped the juvenile home, but drowned trying to swim the Mississippi.

They should always be called out, *No matter what,* she says, and the others quiet down about whatever bad blood and sadness they know. Pearl Wayne and Mamie D come with John Hogan and Dwight Sellers, who says nothing Harry Lee did right could stand up to the bad liquor they sold out of the trunks of their cars way back then. Melba Sellers up and scolds them all for comparing troubles like it mattered.

They are all coming now. Gilbert limps to the church house and tells me it is never locked. I can go in anytime, but *use the side door, it's the one 'ats open.* I turn the knob and there is pretty Joy Gastineau and Glenna O'Connor skipping, yes skipping up the steps, both annoyed at each other because they wore the same pink dress, though they lived and died fifty years apart. Hessie Willhite and Cletis Setzer are all waiting with hats in hand, still arguing over that bottomland.

But when I open the door, the low white ceiling and the plain walls and all the empty seats silence them. They enter quiet-like, take places assigned by their families. Delaney Nunn is the one who acts as preacher, tickled that he is *no nun* but a priest of sorts. We sit for a few, and of course Heather and Joshua Askins, late as always, dart in the door. Little Eva Huff and Homer Swyzer hang just outside, rubbing their shyness and toes in the clay.

When our true and living Maddie plays the piano for them, Dixie Ragon leads in a song to which I have never heard the words. They all join in, and those even-older folks—the ones whose names are gone, whose places on the hillside are marked by plain Missouri stones with no names and no years and no

story we know, though it might have been from the time of
this state's great troubles and failings—rise up from the yellow
grasses, crowd in through the windows, more wisp than ghost,
but truer to the witnessing for being less. They can sing, too, if
given our thought.

We stay there awhile, us living folks, and listen to their
voices rise and fade, their prayers, which are really one prayer,
written on the preacher cloth draped over the battered lectern.
"Remember to pray," is what they say over and over in their
amazement, their heartache. It does not mean what we think
it does. It means remember to say, out loud, what we need
and how much we love each other. They stand there in their
river of names and sing the old songs of time and time past,
bringing the river inside in a flood of hymnal cacophony and
memory We are not afraid. Do you know that it is a pleasure
to stand among them? After a while we stand up and go outside again and close the door of the church house that was
only used for funerals.

On the way out, we pass the Wiests. Anna Mryleen drowned
when she was six. Her mama died on the train trestle just three
years later. She tossed the baby she held to her man, and some
say she could have saved herself, but those with us, the Cowl-
ings, who knew her, shake their heads and say no, it was no
good.

And so they all lead us to the fence. As we leave, Gilbert
leans down on one of the big stones, "These are good," he
says. "Cuz they don't turn over easy." And all the spirits nod
and wish us well and wave good-bye, and they place their
hands over their eyes for all that sun and watch until we've disappeared over their rise, back to spring pastures and the black
cows sunning themselves, back to fish in the creek, back to

imaginings, however mistaken, that prove they lived, that they had hearts that beat, stories that we learn to tell through our own strange dreams.

Before we leave the Huzzah River the next day, I stop again at Justin's and watch the fish inside his glass river one last time. I watch them float and hear the fading echo of the voices inside me. They are going now. Justin tells me about his system for keeping the water aerated, the level of nitrogen down, a filter he's built in the woods. He knows when the balance is not right, for then the eyes of the fish distort, bulge, and some go blind. *Got to keep the balance,* he says, touching the glass, that clear boundary between the river we live and the river inside. And then we climb into the Jeep and drive out of those northern Ozarks, out of the place so fraught with floods of history that all you have to do is call a name and they come out of the dirt and weeds, walk out of the rivers where they have just been immersed and cleansed.

An Essay of Supposition

Suppose that a place could come to represent a part of you, or that you could associate parts of your self with specific places, that you could say *this place means my heart.* My heart would be in Michigan, on that farm where I grew up in Oceana County, on the western knuckle of that mitten-shaped peninsula. That place is where, by birth and necessity, the heartbeat pulses that moves everything forward in my world. Or suppose imagination could be assigned a location. That would be the home David and I built together outside the village of Empire, Michigan, where a house and a writing cabin perch on a ravine and stare into the deciduous woods and sometimes, when the season is right, all the way to the lake. There, thought, words, spirit, and love combine to give me essential imagination, fully embodied.

Or suppose we are led to places that represent various states of being. That you might find a place to bring you rest (a mountain), retreat from work (a river), wildness (the ocean), or perhaps a place that opens your mind to learning (an island), or finally a place that is holy with beauty or a place that makes you so honest you see things the way they are instead of the way you want them to be.

Suppose you could do it with your soul. What place would represent it? If there were a place that meant my soul, where would it be?

It would have to be something I realize over time.

It would have started years ago with a dear friend Betsy, who somehow knew that when David and I married in the dead of winter, we didn't have time for a real honeymoon, didn't have a real place to go away. So she offered her cottage in Maine. *A simple place,* she said. *On the ocean. A belated honeymoon.*

So that summer, we travel to New Hampshire first, David to study mathematics at the University of New Hampshire and me to write. We live in a little apartment in New Market, a second-floor walk-up, awkwardly furnished, right across from the fire department. And after David goes off to classes, I try to write, though as the summer wears on, I know only that I'm writing poorly. I have this little room at the front of the apartment that looks across the street, and all summer those boys are trying out new fire trucks for the town of New Market, trucks so loud and rumbling that when they start up the engine and the pumps, the windows tremble. Those boys, cute as they are, are noisy, too, especially the ones who take the late shift, drinking coffee at midnight, telling dirty jokes, and I look across and wonder why I can't write anything but cheerful, dishonest letters. Every time they take one of those trucks around the block and run that siren, I discover I haven't been writing worth shit and delete the whole day's work. So by the time August rolls around, and we can actually accept Betsy's offer, I am fed up, and I wish I could just go home, but David says, *Come on,* and runs his finger along the line of my chin.

So suppose you drive up the coast of Maine and into Brunswick, a sweet town with a bar they call the Barking Spider, and turn on route 123, which scuttles down the Harpswell Neck, a long finger of land that runs southeast into the Atlantic, and then you're bumping down the two-track, avoiding the potholes, and then on down a steep, almost washed-out driveway to a spit you didn't expect thrust at the ocean. And you stare at a cottage sitting a couple dozen feet from the blue-green sound, all gray shingles and deck. You climb out of the car in silence, and the air is different here, as is the light; it's cool gray and soft, but quick, too. The tide is high, and a heron swings overhead so low you can hear its wings. You unlock the door and walk in, and though it's rustic, there are clear windows in every direction, and you can watch the ocean, and you look out at the sound and the islands, and you listen for the fire engines, and they are not there.

Suppose you and your husband spend a week there, and it is foggy almost every day—not the kind of fog you dread but the kind that drifts and has layers, that moves like something alive. Sometimes the fog clears, and you stare at the islands, and then it closes again, and you stare at each other. Suppose you walk to Dick's Dock for lobster, and you bring them back and boil them, and your husband laughs because you, the farm girl, can't be in the room when he drops Bonnie and Clyde into the boiling water.

Suppose you wake up with the early light on this most eastern end of the time zone and hear the lobster boats chugging out to pull in their traps. You watch them, even in the misty noon when they throw the bait off, and the gulls swarm and scream, and you think maybe you are inside a poem. And suppose you sit late at night in front of the big windows and your husband rubs your feet and tells you stories about his father that you have never heard, and then you know you are inside a poem. Suppose you do not write for two or three days, and then one day the words begin to pour out of you.

Then suppose you have a chance to return to New England every summer for a few years, so you see lots of places in Maine, lots of rocky beaches, and you learn to know this coast a little, Popham and Stone Coast, Wildwood, where Virginia Lockwood lives, but you always come back to Betsy's place because the light that close is right, and she is generous with it and seems to know that people need it. You learn to rely on that light that cleans you out, and the fog and the ocean, most of all the ocean. You never have trouble writing here. You never have trouble with a small room that looks over a noisy street. There is always the ocean, which you learn is a room that never gets small. The windows never tremble unless it is from the wind, and then the trembling is all good.

Suppose over time, you find the five boulders that mark high tide and low tide, and you learn to read the charts, and you walk to Pott's Point and watch the osprey practice. Suppose there is a night all the grad students from school come and your husband hauls pots of seawater up for the boiling of steamers and mussels. The great Thomas Mosher table is laden with shells and dead soldiers and around it so much laughter you nearly wet your pants. Or there is a Fourth of July with stars-and-stripes tablecloths and people from the neighborhood, and you watch fireworks and talk on the deck and stay up way too late watching the lights on Bailey's Island come across the water right at you. And what about the sunsets that travel miles across the sound and through your window, catch you just right so that you see it a dozen times in the surface of the sea, even though you are looking straight north. What about the time you see the seals playing just offshore and want to be one?

You bring small white shells back to the Midwest and set them on your windowsills.

Suppose one night, a winter night, the phone rings, and it is Betsy, and she tells you the cottage is burning right then (arson, they think) and will burn to the ground, and all that soft light drains out of you, and you stare at the white shells until they seem disembodied, and you can't talk for long because you know you'll lose it, and when you hang up, you do. But then you go to the computer and find every poem you ever wrote there and write some more and send them all to her.

Suppose she rebuilds the cottage, using the same floorplan, but adds that downstairs bathroom she always wanted, and though she's lost so much, including the great old silver and her grandmother's paintings, she makes it so she can live there year 'round, and the new fireplace has stone eyes, and when you finally go again, you see that she has done something with the light, something to bring it back, and the wind is fresh and moody again.

One summer we help Betsy reshingle the storage shed; the one side is charred from the fire and needs to be resided. It is a day that feels like being inside a Wyeth painting, all cool color and dry grass and long views and a melancholy that will not hurt, and so we tap in the cedar shakes and move in tandem and tap, tap, and we hear rhythms coming back off the waves, and I figure out how to put them in a poem. And when David and I are building our own home in Michigan, and we have been living without plumbing and a kitchen for a while, Betsy sends money for the plane, and I come all the way back east, and she lets me cook in the new kitchen all weekend long, and it rains so hard we have to wade through two feet of water to get wood from the shed, and the cottage is like a castle in a sea, and we sit around the fireplace and drink wine and hear the sea vibrate just outside, so close and fierce, and I love it even more. The next year there is a hurricane, but the cottage survives, though she has to rebuild the seawall.

And suppose Betsy, now a long and tried-true friend, loses first her mom and then her dad. She builds a garden in back of the cottage, just where the land rises away from the sea, with slab-rock walls and dozens of Grutendorst roses that her grandmother's family developed generations ago and that my own family calls the seven sisters, the ones I grew up with but thought I'd lost forever until Betsy. And over time, I try to write about the place, thrust out in the ocean like it is, and how it makes me think and feel, but it's never right, and I decide it's because nothing happens here. There is no narrative line to follow an arc; there is some other structure working, something less linear and clear I'll have to find. I never do.

What if there comes a year, the year after you stop bleeding every month, and you have worked too hard and faced too many crises, and you feel you don't know yourself and can't get pen to paper for the work, and you come alone to Maine and she lets you make a desk of boards on the second floor where you can write. You sleep longer than you have in years, and write and walk, sometimes with her and sometimes alone. You watch the light and keep thinking you see something in it, something peripheral that is there, like looking at stars—

sometimes you see them better sideways.

At night you walk down the ridge to the ocean, and you stare out and try to figure out what it is that you feel, and why, though you can write so easily here, you can not put to words what the light is doing, how the colors shift, how in the fog that drifts almost every morning, there are memories and histories of love and loss as long as time. You try to put to words how it works, but every time, it feels trite and small compared to what you feel here. You watch the waves and look as far as you can. One day you turn and catch yourself in the mirror and finally see who you are now.

Suppose you don't like to say to anyone that this place is where you come closest to your soul, that once in a while you think that's what you see rising in the spray, or shifting in the mist. You don't like to give that much power to a place, that much possibility to a place where nothing happens. You don't like to admit that when you sit on the deck of her house and look to the moon rising over that glimmering Atlantic, that when you turn your face to a wind or watch the salt-laced rain smack the roses and you feel wildness shouting over the seawall, or on a calm day you count the rocks all the way down to the lowest tide, something fills you up with the longing for words to say, but you can never wield them precisely enough to say what you know and how you know it.

Suppose all that were true, is true. Wouldn't you return and try again, drawn to this place where you can almost see, almost know the inside of something that must be oceanic and moody and melancholic and sparkling and cold and full of life. Wouldn't you keep supposing, keep trying to say how a place, how a place can take a shape inside, reside there, and when you are in that place, something in you comes out and spreads wide and becomes liquid and wind.

Finding (My) America

Library Tour, Michigan

I. BUNTING

I am packing our old Mazda, trusting its hundred thousand plus miles to the road yet again. David throws in my frayed blue suitcase; I toss in the unmatched red garment bag. I turn to him and move into his arms and we kiss deeply and hold each other for a long time in the dappled June light that spills over our small north woods home. I'll be gone less than a week, but I am rarely alone in a life now inextricably, fortuitously coupled.

We kiss again, and he pulls away to look at my face, but does not let go. He is worried about me, not about the travel, but about a sadness that has crept into my spirit lately. It is a sadness that has to do with the world, with the weight of the world. We chuckle about my cliché, the *weight of the world* in what can only be called a lucky life, but it is the only way I have been able to describe it. And though it could be self-indulgent, it doesn't feel that way, this sadness he can do nothing about, except that his holding me holds my uneasiness at bay for a few moments. Then I slip out of his embrace, leave my unruly gardens, my cluttered home and our opinionated cats to his care. I climb into this reliable car, drive the dusty gravel road down the hill and turn, not west toward my beloved Lake Michigan as is my habit, but east on M-72 to the interior roads of this peninsula state. My journey: four visits to that most American of American phenomena, the small-town library.

To my surprise, my book, *Pulling Down the Barn,* became a Michigan Notable Book, a designation given by the Library of Michigan. As part of the honor, I have been invited to read at four different libraries in the state. The Library of Michigan Foundation, an organization profound in its goodness, supports the writers who receive this award with an honorarium for each library visit. Authors are matched to libraries, large and small, all over the state. It seems to me an excellent use of the private money that is raised for such projects. When given the list of requesting libraries, I ask for those in rural communities in the northern half of the state, thinking that my book about a rural childhood will offer more common ground for those audiences than for readers nearer Detroit, Flint, the southern counties.

I care deeply for libraries. To most of the world, I identify myself as a nerd by saying that. I probably am—a nerd for valuing books, for reading them, for loving to hold them, smell them, and turn their pages, for revering the places they take me, as well as the places they are housed. Those places of quiet reading, reflection, places where both knowledge and imagination live. Too, I am a nerd for worrying about a warming lake and a warming planet, native versus invasive plants (what will we do with all that tufted knapweed and those zebra mussels?), the destruction of soil through poor farming practices, the loss of songbirds, receding glaciers, sick honeybees, the proliferation of the ash borer, unhealthy feedlots and unhealthy food; a nerd for thinking about the motives of both car bombers and congress, for worrying about my nieces and nephews who have recently lost a soldier friend in Iraq—their first death of this kind but one that recalled my long-past losses of friends in Vietnam.

I am worrying about my country.

I drive east through the rolling hills of Leelanau County, heading for Kalkaska, my first stop, noticing porches already hung with Independence Day red, white, and blue bunting. Do they think about our country too? Is mine different from theirs? What does it mean to be an ordinary person, a teacher by trade, a writer by art, a farmer at heart, and a citizen of a nation among many nations?

I drive, telling myself not to get too caught up in thinking, that I have work to do, and it is good work. I will read to people from my book about my farm-rooted childhood in Michigan. What could be sweeter and, in some ways, more American? And I tell myself this journey is a microcosmic version of another American experience, the legendary road trip. After all, it is a journey in a car (albeit decidedly unsporty), out on the open roads of my beloved state (so it's only one of fifty), to places I have never been (shows what a homebody I've become). Still, I'm a little pumped-up with grandiosity, thinking of Lewis and Clark, the Conestoga wagon, the airstream; of Least Heat Moon and *Motorcycle Maintenance* and Route 66. Though my miles are for the literary—some would say nerdy—purpose of a book tour in my home state, my route will include at least a few of those legendary blue highways. Like Steinbeck, I will become newly acquainted with the "People"—that particular stripe of Americans called Michiganders (the name given us by Abraham Lincoln). I will sleep in strange beds. And like all road trippers, I hold a fledgling hope in the gesture of the road trip, in the notion that in motion I will find an antidote, an answer. Maybe not—after all, I'm a middle-aged, married, menopausal woman, not a twenty-something Bohemian, and I have lost the blazing optimism I carried with me when I actually did live the Bohemian life. But what *will* happen out there? These are miles I cover with a heightened sense of receptivity—the pilgrim's adventure.

There is something else. When I set out alone on M-72 west, braving a thousand miles or so of Michigan roads, a ferry, the Mackinac Bridge, and a rollercoaster of moods and perceptions that bring me to my knees, I hope I will be changed.

II. KALKASKA

Kalkaska is the name of our state soil, a course mix of sandy loam and gravel found nowhere else in the world. It is also the name of this small town, where, despite being namesake of soil, there exists a history of oil and the military industrial complex. Wells and forts. Like bad lovers, both have abandoned the town. It shows. Where once streets bustled with uniformed men and their families, with oil hustlers and their contracts, the sidewalks now are populated with people "just passing through," and the once grand downtown hotel is in disrepair. Storefronts are closed and sprawl squalls at the outskirts like the disorderly stepchild it is. Still, the world is steadier than we think, and the celebrated trout sculpture, a fifteen-foot replica complete with glistening rainbow, graces the highway for Trout Festival, a beacon of community spirit. The corner of U.S. 131 and M-72 still lures travelers and locals alike with one of the best open fruit markets in the region. A few years ago, the school district stopped busing (no money), but those same schools graduate good students every year.

But will anyone in this town come to hear me read? Despite the integrity of its working population, it is not a town noted as a cultural mecca. Will they come to their library to hear the visiting author? It is the question every author asks, for in a world of Netflix, iPods, and Comcast, books can seem, despite their quiet power, simply quaint. And a book about rural life and farms? I know from experience it is not unusual to read for fewer than ten people, and, indeed, I have put my heart into reading for as few as two if they had that look of attention that requires a tale. As I push the speed limit down the treeless stretch of highway at the center of town, I suspect I am about to do it again.

Kalkaska missed the Carnegie era, and an unassuming one-story runs smack against the highway with parking abutted on the side. I rush in, breathless and minutes late, to stacks crowded with people. Many people. A couple of dozen people have crowded into short rows of plastic chairs in a shoebox-shaped alcove, small enough to be intimate, large enough for a real crowd. Their faces are marked by ordinary concerns: late house payments and new babies. Most are dressed in the common midwestern uniform of T-shirts or flowered blouses, slacks or jeans, and practical, often battered shoes with ties or Velcro. A smattering in business attire, out of place. They chat softly, greeting each other.

"Hello, Jerry, how ya doin?"

"Oh, be better if I could get the hay in."

"What you doing here, then?"

"Well, it ain't rainin' yet.

"No need to rush."

A young mother hands off her toddler to an older woman who murmurs, "It's all right, I'll take her out if she gets fussy."

And as the child sets up a squeal, the younger woman answers, "Want to do that now?"

Banter good-natured and tart as homemade cider made from sour apples. That they are comfortable in this space is my first clue that the library culture is alive and well. As I unpack books, the women rein the children in from the kid's corner and check on next week's story hour, tomorrow's car pool. The teachers wave—some know me from writing workshops—and a handful of men stand in back, leaning on their elbows over the waist-high stacks, their hands locking and unlocking in front of them. *Just came in with the wife, you know.* This is as close as they will come.

But they have come; they have all come.

A librarian with dark curls, Kathleen Mosher, whispers how happy she is about the crowd and then offers a warm introduction. I step to the front of the small space and begin the ceremonial part of a reading by acknowledging the work of the librarians and the Friends of the Library. I speak of the library tour and what it means to writers, and then, without microphone or podium, holding my book in hands that shake for an unsettling minute, I open my voice to them.

This is where it begins for me, in the proud and frightening moment when I finally look at them and begin to read. In a library. The place where entertainment and information is free, where quiet and not-so-quiet rooms house the amazement of reading. And because I have been listening to the news and thinking about my country, it occurs to me as I stand there:

in how many countries would I be forbidden to read my story about competing with my brothers. About a woman driving a tractor. About the moment of leaving Eden. No, not leaving it, but not belonging there at all. The sentences come, one after another, as easily and freely as brushing my hair.

Tell me what happens to people when they are read to. It happens to me, too, but I need someone from the outside to look at and explain it. I sense that when I am reading or being read to, if it is done with skill, the energy shifts and flits between the reader and the read to, and evolves into something just short of reading each other's minds. Do a group of people all listening to the same story—a story that has taken them not to spirituality as prayer might, but to the internal realm of imagination where all of us, through language, enter another world—create a unity there, in that place, that we find in no other communal experience?

Is that what our faces look like there?

The retiree with a pretty pink blouse and roller-curled hair nods and chuckles at the awkwardness of learning to drive a tractor. The men, their hands still now, attend deeply when I read about the tractor accident, the damaged truck—they know exactly what it means to damage equipment. Some tear up when I read how my father consoled me, and when I arrive at the end, where, though it means hard things to me, I know who I am, they clap. It is always a surprise.

Before the applause is done, the hands rise like sprouts.

I have learned that if you scrape the surface of my state just a bit, pry under the auto industries of Detroit, the furniture history of Grand Rapids, and all the varied manufacturing, you will find the farms still remembered. Most of us are the children or grandchildren of farmers. My story has touched that larger memory and it lifts its head, awake again. For a little

while, in that plain space surrounded by books, we know ourselves in that older light.

They do not ask questions. Instead, they tell their own
lives, associating my memories freely with theirs. One woman
speaks of driving a John Deere for ten hours straight to prepare a field for seed. One tells of getting stuck in mud and
waiting a month for the field to dry while every other planting
was delayed to loss. Another speaks of the PTO tractor accident that killed his uncle.

I close my book and listen, sometimes tearing up myself.

I am no nostalgia freak. I do not long for the "good old
days," when hardship was denied or romanticized on a Wal-
tonesque scale. I do not believe in Norman Rockwell as much
as I do Edward Hopper. I know hardships were real and people
sometimes died brutally from the inevitable machinery acci-
dents on farms where safety and health were the least-consid-
ered practices in the face of the fields' demands. Yet there is
something to be learned by the telling of these stories, some
reclamation, not of a way of life, for that is truly gone, but
perhaps of the spirit of resourcefulness. These are the stories
to help us in the utterly changed world we live in now. I see in
their faces that these people are strengthened by the telling.
For a moment we know each other again.

Then, the men drum their fingers on the Formica-topped
stacks. Grandma brings the baby back. Arms unfold, legs un-
cross, feet tap. When the cookies appear, it is all over but the
signing. One of the things I learn to trust about all Friends of
the Library organizations is that none of these good people
have forgotten the role of sweets in the world. Each time I
visit a library, cookies and sweet bars, along with strong coffee
and sugary punch will grace a side table covered with a flowered cloth, set with a vase of daisies or some seasonal pink.

Whether it be meals or meetings, church or stories, we cel-
ebrate completion with cookies.

Before I leave, the librarian takes my hand and leads me to
a teenaged girl, squashed into a chair at a back table. Trisha is
her name. She shyly tells me she likes my book, and that *she
likes to write.* She is trying, but it is hard. Her mother, standing
near, interrupts to tell me that her daughter writes beautiful
poetry. I look at Trisha's face. There is a desperateness to the
lanky hair hanging over her eyes, the heaviness of her body. I
suggest a writing group, and she nods but I can see in her eyes
that she does not think that possible. I know this look. I give
her the titles of handbooks. I tell her to seek a teacher, to read
good poetry, the best she can find. I write down poets' names.
Finally I give her my card and ask her to send me something.
She takes it in her large hands, and I see her nails bitten to
bleeding. She stuffs the card in her back jeans pocket. She nods
and promises that she will. Shy thanks. Then, mother trailing,
she's out the door, hope and resignation warring in her face.

Which will win? I know already she will not send me anything, but I know too she may hoard the card, tucking it into
some diary she may fill. I know few in her school will know
how to respond to the first awkward poem she will attempt
after reading Emily Dickinson or James Wright. She will chew
her nails and try to become someone else. I know all this because I was like her.

What will happen to her in a place where, as good as the
education may be, there will be little help for a developing
poet? I survived for a long time on books, on libraries, those
pockets of safety in a world that did not always appreciate
poetry. Will she? In this small town, will they guide her until
she finds the teacher she needs? Will she find friends who will
speak of words and different worlds in those hallways where

the boys will call her *fatty*? For a moment, I imagine her finding a job working for cash under the table in the open fruit market. She's a little bored, smuggles a copy of William Carlos Williams's poems (*I have eaten the plums . . .*) into a box of tomatoes, or gets scolded for reading when she was supposed to be unpacking apples, but then the woman behind the deli loans her Robert Frost, and she reads "Out, Out . . ." for the first time and cries as she sorts the first cherries of the season.

I hope for a scene like that.

When I sign the last book, one of the Friends thrusts a paper plate laden with cookies *for the road*. I thank the librarian one last time and carry my plate to the car. When I pull onto U.S. 131 and head north to the bridge, dusk is already settling. The air is cool, the light low gold over the grasses. I drive the miles, thinking of the reading, thinking about how to better respond to their stories. Despite the potato farmer's warm handshake and thanks as I left, I wish I could quell the sadness about what we've lost with more than this short-lived connection.

As I drive north, the light dies over the woods and fields. I follow end-of-day pickups until they pull into their gravel driveways, where mercury lights flicker over yards pocked with rusty snowmobiles and plastic toys. I pass through the small towns of Mancelona and Alden before I cut east to I-75 where the places become merely names and exit numbers one passes too quickly to know: Vanderbilt, Wolverine. The stars are out when, near Indian River, I pull into an *open-for-summer* log lodge and rent a room whose primary characteristics are musty linen and damp air, where my allergies kick in and my loneliness for David tucks into the cold dark of the sheets. This part of the road I always forget until I am living it, this bedding down without a partner, without a sense of place. The road's essential loneliness. The pride I felt from the reading slips out from under me, and I sleep restlessly, dreaming their faces, Trisha, books flickering under mercury light.

III. DRUMMOND ISLAND

To cross the Mackinac Bridge is to cross history and wild water. It is to be thrilled and frightened, to be intimidated and inspired. Its architecture, the great pillars' majestic suspension swinging gracefully down to the highway, is the stuff of myth. Its height and span, its silhouette, all of it leaves me breathless—all this for two dollars and fifty cents. Hundreds of feet below, Lake Huron spreads out on my right, Lake Michigan on the left; the islands of both lakes float in the distance; and then there is all that immensity written in water.

The bridge unites Michigan's two peninsulas, the state's two rocky hearts, but what I always notice is the water that divides them. Crossing, I live for a moment at the demarcation of two great waters. I drive these five bridge-miles in a state of high attention, so alert that I gasp when my wheels hit the open grid spanning the middle, where the low drone of concrete gives way to a loud thrum. I roll down my window to feel the twenty-degree drop in temperature that marks traveling above big water. Open water. What is the place of suspension between the lakes? What does it mean to drive the road that joins upper and lower, two different peninsulas, to look first toward one lake, then the other? What happens at this water-rushed bridge? A coming together and a boundary? A separation or a joining of places?

When the highway eases down on the other side, I am in the Upper Peninsula, the U.P., the Michigan that some have called the last wilderness, the Michigan of the timber industry, the wild bear, old mines. Copper Country. Or the Silver State—as it was called for a fault line so rich with silver, as well as iron, it built an ore industry, though that same industry now lies nearly fallow. Here, a population reputed to be both independent and self-reliant, full of backwoods wisdom (no matter how faulty) and do-it-yourself determination live on with hunting dogs, fishing poles, chainsaws, and Carhartts at the ready. There are also fine universities: Michigan Tech and Lake Superior State College, among others, swell with students interested in science and mathematics. In the northern deeps of Lake Superior, Isle Royale, with its wolf and moose populations, calls to ecotourists and history-seekers with tales of Ruth Douglas, the first woman to spend a winter there and not lose her sanity.

Hard country, my father would say.

I turn east on M-134, the cutoff for the village of Drummond, on Drummond Island, my next library. The two-lane skirts the southern edge of the eastern Upper Peninsula and allows for a long look down the gullet of Lake Huron. I am far north in my country, within an hour of our Canadian border. All along this shore, inlets open on the rock-pocked sand. Here, people pull into beaches that have only local names and take the ever-cool of Great Lakes currents. I pass a mom bathing her toddler, all soaped up and ready to rinse. I pass a young couple in a sleeping bag, gear strewn around their section of beach like a small maelstrom had roared through just after they finished the bottle of wine.

Appropriately named De Tour Village, the town lies where M-134 stops to skip a mile across the St. Marys River to Drummond Island. De Tour is a cluster of balloon-frame buildings made bright by the morning's sun. There are a few small businesses: garages and gas stations, two real estate companies, a school. Small clapboard houses freshly painted or in need of it. The main drag to the ferry passes the Fog Cutter, a graying American-style diner with Upper Peninsula–style hardy cuisine. Eggs and American fries. Beef hash and packaged Hollandaise. Pasties with carrots and turnips. And gravy or ketchup for everything. De Tour sports a coastal bustle, but the ferry seems the actual center, the only way to Drummond Island and the village of Drummond.

To get there, one must leave Michigan's mainland, cross the De Tour Passage on the car ferry (no suspension bridge here) and pick up the highway on the island. I edge the Mazda toward this freighter-like contraption of iron and solidity, De Tour Ferry IV, a heavy ark designed to take in cars on this side and release them on the other. The channel here is not wide, but so deep that the great ships can pass between Drummond and the Upper Peninsula, cutting hours and expense on their way north to Sault St. Marie. I am early for the hourly run, but already a dozen or so vehicles are waiting. I follow the tight lines and arrows nearly to the bumper of the SUV in front of me. Within minutes, thirty-six vehicles line up like orderly blocks fitted into a box. We are on a ship, but it feels like a parking lot.

The sheet of red-painted steel that acts as ramp pivots upward and becomes barrier between us and this wild if not so wide water. The deck hands seal the ferry, blow the great whistle, and then the engine throbs, and the ship moves placidly over the black silks of the passage.

Most people, unimpressed, stay in their cars to drink morning coffee or spread a newspaper over the steering wheel. I squeeze out of mine and slide through a maze of automobiles to lean over the side of the boat. The water is an opaque navy today, not the almost Caribbean blue-green of the shoreline inlets, but steely with depth. Though clear, the air over the water is brisk. A burly deckhand with a rough beard and rolling gait tips his hat, sells me my ticket for twelve dollars. I ask him how long it takes to get over. *Five minutes or so.* And how long to the town of Drummond. *Five minutes or so.* And the library from there? *Five minutes or so.* And how long to my bed and breakfast, beyond the town. *Oh that one, fifteen minutes.* Or so. I am grateful for the variation. I lean over the rail, and the wind, freshwater sharp, pulls my hair out of its combs and tangles it—along with my heart.

Oh, this water.

In Michigan, one travels always under the influence of fresh water—two inland seas, Lake Michigan and Lake Huron or, if one is traveling the Upper Peninsula, one drives in the northern shadow of Lake Superior, the deepest and largest of these sweetwater seas. These lakes are weathermakers, dispensing moods as varied, threatening, or serene as the great oceans. But they are not an endless resource, and these days, they are, for all their depth and vastness, vulnerable to industry, pollution, a series of invasive species, and rising temperatures. I stare over the water and wonder how much longer the lakes can live as we know them. As much as the highway, the farms and towns, water is a part of me. Its liquid richness runs in me; it's the true blood of my state.

But here is this island looming out of these waters, 136 square miles, gleaming with cedar and stone. Despite its unsleek bulk, the ferry cuts quickly through the waves and slows only once, to allow what looks like an oversized coast guard cutter to pass before us. Within minutes De Tour Ferry IV's low hum alters, and our captain pulls expertly to a small but

solid landing. The steel gate falls, men lock the ramp, and I join
the queue of cars bumping slowly onto an island where I have
never been.

This time, it's not about the library.

At the Four Corners, Drummond's obvious town center,
a billboard-style signpost sports dozens of arrows pointing in
four directions to every resort, campsite, restaurant, fudge-
maker, and B and B. As arranged, I meet Joy Cameron, the
friendly woman in charge of the library at Drummond Island
Realty. She gives me directions to the bed-and-breakfast where
I will stay. *Why don't you go and get settled? Just take the road east.*
She'll see me tonight at the reading, but *Gee, I'm not sure how
many will come*—a baby shower at the same time for one of
their circle of friends and—*Well, you know how it is.* Sometimes
it's not about the reading, not about me, but about a baby
shower in a small community, where babies and their mothers
are the story.

In the early nineteen hundreds, the ramshackle building that
is now the Wayfarer's Mart was a general market for the island
and then during the last couple of decades, a restored bed-and-
breakfast, an antique store, and a tea shop where Carol Martin,
a sturdy woman with clear but tired eyes once served elegant
Sunday teas. The pioneer-style front porch invites me into the
high-ceilinged community rooms. In the back outside, I see a
bedraggled tongue of dock that thrusts into Scammon Cove.

Carol works for a newspaper now and hasn't time for the
antiques (most sold on consignment) or the teas, but she says
that I am welcome to look around.

"Sorry about the clutter."

Since she closed the antiques business years ago, she says,
not everyone has picked up *these collectibles,* even though she

ran the sale for a long time and called all the owners afterward.

"I still let them be." She glances over the worn-out garden tools and the partial sets of crystal dishware.

She settles me in a bedroom overlooking the cove, touches the bed with pride, pointing out the soft mattress *made right here in the U.P.* The room is long and narrow, decorated with flowered paper. There is a window seat for *staring at the water.* And then she too tells me about the same shower tonight for one of their island friends—they all know each other on this island—and she might have to work on the paper—

"So even though I'm interested in hearing you read, I might duck out. Nothing personal."

Carol excuses herself to mow the lawn, and I take up her suggestion to wander the yawning rooms. An antiques and collectibles shop is an amazingly American experience. Here, all the accoutrements of the Settlement era, Depression era, War and Postwar eras, all the way to the plastics of the sixties—still for sale. Shelves and tables laden with chipped bean crocks, discolored kitchen utensils, filigreed but short-circuited lamps, old books and old boots, cutlery and crockery, cabinet radios and ancient plows. Vinyl 45s! All of it gathered and for sale. We do not use or need this stuff anymore, but in our entrepreneurial spirit, we try to convince others they do. So we try to sell it. Or trade it. My acquisitiveness is cast off only to become my acquisitiveness again. I do not need any of these things, but I enjoy them with such . . . attachment. I want them, or some thing. Again. I finger the faded beauty and utility of the last century. Is it abundance, even old and broken abundance, that triggers the impulse to collect? Or is it that I am on new territory—this amazing island—and I want to make a connection to it? I open a Hardy Boys mystery, check the rim of a pickling crock, lift a rose-bedecked teacup.

But as much as I love the piecemeal review of history through the random picking up and putting down of everything from chamber pots to gold-rimmed sherry glasses, what I want more is the story behind the thing, the tale of getting or giving up the item. Was the chamber pot used for old Uncle Harry after he fell off the haymow and broke both legs? Were the sherry glasses sold after that preacher man came through town and Grandma Victoria was persuaded that sherry was a sin? Wouldn't that be a tale? And my mind is off and running. She wore rings and a green feather boa . . . I want a connection that tells a story of the place or the people. That's what inspires my collecting.

When Carol stalls the mower and comes in for water, I ask her about local artists. She thinks a minute and then tells me about Skip Benson, a man who makes pots from clay found only here on Drummond.

"Does he have a shop?"

"Works at his house."

"Who carries his pottery?"

"You go to his house."

"Oh. Is he an okay guy?"

"Quiet, but yeah, he's okay."

After I manage to get a number, I call Skip Benson and ask if, after the reading, I might be able to look at his work. After a long silence, he says yes.

As predicted, attendance is sparse, and because the room is large, the crowd seems a mere smattering, though when I count fifteen, I realize that's plenty for a reading. Joy, the librarian, mentions the party again with apologies.

Still, when the reading begins, these listeners turn toward me with attentive eyes. A couple turn up their hearing aids, and I tell myself to remember to project in this bigger room. And again my memory-story, this time about haying and storms, triggers their own stories. These people are islanders and speak, not of farms, but of other kinds of lost land, lost opportunities. One says, "They tried rice here." One says he came from the "thumb area," where "You stick anything in that soil—it comes up big—but not here." One man says it's easier to fish. I mention that fishing is also a form of harvesting. He nods, and then he tells me, "My people lived off the fish until the fishing rights got screwed up by the damned Indians. No fish now," he says angrily, "not a one."

The remark springs up sharp as unexpected metal. Before I can think to mention other threats that cause fish populations to plummet—cormorants, invasive zebra mussels, rampant botulism, even sports fishing—Joy diplomatically announces refreshments. I sigh and turn to sign books. The islanders are generous with their praise. Joy is generous with the cookie plate, this time graced with my favorites: peanut butter and chocolate no-bakes. But despite the sweets, I feel both annoyed and bereft, wondering what would make the ex-fisherman reconsider his statement? More important, could I have been a vehicle for change? I want to argue him down, make him see that the issues are more complicated and difficult than the *damned Indians*—though fishing rights may play a role in those complications. But even as I sit in the parking lot and mutter to his imaginary being, I know that offending him would only make him more adamant. What would have opened his mind? And why was I reticent to pursue a gentler conversation?

My own lack of courage?

Skip answers the front door of the double-wide set back on a gravel two-track from the road. In the dim light I can see he has a large head and sharp eyes and a gruff voice accented by a place I cannot identify. When I introduce myself, he nods, says, "They're in the trailer, but there's no light out there. I got flashlights. You want to come out?" He motions for me to follow. I wonder at my sanity, but I follow him through his house, out onto a small deck and across the yard toward a trailer the color and texture of light rust. Though the dusk-long light still holds, the trailer sits back, among woods. It will be darker there. It occurs to me I haven't told anyone where I am going. I should stop, ask him to bring the pots back to the car, or stay in a place where there is light. I should turn and run.

What am I doing here?

Why am I afraid?

Oh dear. Whose bigotry is showing now? And with that, I remember that he is an islander; his life is lived here, and people know him. I am country myself; this is something I can trust. The door squeals open, and I step up into the unsteady vibration of a small trailer not quite stabilized. Walls stripped of cabinetry and appliances have been lined with shelves to form a galley-shaped interior. Twilight spills in from the yard and silhouettes hundreds of bowls, vases, mugs. The flash blooms on the pots: a warm brown, muted green, mustard. Earth tones.

What am I really doing here? Acquiring an artist-shaped artifact, a connection, something to hold my own failings. I am finding the story, a story of the place and of an artist, but also of me, because I am in it, making it happen too, and this one is a little sad, for I have not addressed an issue that should have been addressed, and now I cannot, and so the emptiness of the bowl I will choose is also my own.

Skip watches me, calm and self-possessed. I pick up one after another and hold it carefully while he shines the light. The bowls are as thin and light as is possible without a mold, and he knows their value—they are not cheap. I ask him about the native clay and he tells me that he goes to the bluffs and finds pockets. He holds his hands in a cup, *like this,* he says. His hands are thick with an independence that throwing pots and digging rare clay have given him. He lets me pick up one piece after another. He holds the light as I run my fingers over many, touching the glazed surface.

I pick three that nest, one inside another, shiny terra cotta rimmed by green, ochre and red trim, bowls that signal both utility and aesthetics. He wraps them in newspaper and snugs them into a canned-goods box and folds the flaps. I write a check, and he looks at it for a long time, longer than he has looked at me at any time in this exchange. Is it his turn to be distrustful? Or is it that he cannot believe he is paid for the work? He folds it into his wallet. I thank him and he nods, already looking back to his pots, adjusting the ones I have moved. In the shadow of the flashlight, his hands are almost unnatural, separate from him. They know things about where clay lies on this island. They know how to make a bowl that will hold a small sadness, a large loneliness, even a lack of courage, and keep it from spilling.

IV. THE ALVAR

The next morning I bid good-bye to Carol and her china-laden sideboards, dusty fireplaces, rug whackers and potato peelers. I lug my bags past the chipped set of mismatched crystal wine goblets (tempting) and the crosscut saw (even more so) and dump my stuff (plenty already) back into the Mazda. I thank her and follow her directions to Maxton Road.

"You'll know when you get there," she says. "It's wild."

I do know when I get there, but wild is not the word.

Over the years, I have found many places within places. Sometimes I think they hold the distilled experience of the larger place that cradles them—as an alpine meadow holds the essential vitality of a huge mountain—or they contrast with the surrounding place, defining by contrast—as the deep river caves of Puerto Rico define that island more clearly than the density of heavily populated San Juan. The place within the place may be a heart within a larger body, or the iridescent hollowness inside the bubble. But here I find something else, both a geological essence and an emptiness. The word *place* does not quite fit because the setting is so singular it defies the idea of place—it opens the imagination and spreads out too broadly for language—and yet it is place in its truest form.

Drummond Island's most rare place is the alvar's flat, otherworldly wonder. Past Papin's Resort and Alvin's Landing, tree-lined miles past where Maxton Road's blacktop becomes gravel, I drive out to where the surface of the world changes, or rather where there ceases to be a surface as I understand it. It extends east and west for miles.

Three or four hundred million years or so ago, the seas receded, perhaps several times, and over millennia the glaciers seduced and then scraped clean what was left, until finally this, a revelation of the planet itself. What is bared are not the granites or volcanic rock of Michigan's mountain ranges, but a bone-colored sheet of softer stone that underpins this quadrant of the Great Lakes. Even our geological past is made of what water left, compressed shell and plant life, a limestone liturgy written in glacial scrape over these flats. The limestone layer, which in the rest of the Great Lakes regions drifts from dozens to hundreds of feet below our surface, is the surface here, revealed as a plain, a geological page where a lean layer of beleaguered loam writes an ancient story.

At the Nature Conservancy's kiosk, I park at the edge of an ecosystem so delicate, I can't walk out into it, but only on the roads and paths that are not really roads but simply thoroughfares scraped down. In an alvar, a tulle of webbed root and grasses lace over the limestone bed to anchor what passes for topsoil, a layer of sparse dirt, thin as a veil. Everywhere but the roads, the flats are graced by this fine layer of ragged debris, enough to support the most fragile of ecosystems, which in keeping with the wry ironies of nature, is bedecked with rare beauty and unexpected formality.

I walk a road surface that is not tar and chip, not asphalt, not even gravel, but an epidermis of earth, a limestone layer scarred with the geometry of glaciers. Here the surface of the earth lacks its dressing of soil, has been scraped clean rather than layered on, and this road and the meadow that mats the road's edge do not feel wild as would be expected but rather, because of the linearity of the faults, orderly and methodical, a tidy page where the scrapes and fissures become the glacier's signature, almost like an Asian character, scratched with a stylus of ice.

But the road reveals only a small part of this stone liturgy. The fault lines then continue under the abrupt roadside, under the plate of grassland. Here the trees take up the calligraphy, stippled trunks of stunted poplar crisscross in intricate geometric lines, not randomly scattered, but in rows, dividing the open spaces into almost mathematical plots, leaving the appearance that the only thing free of plan is the flight of a white-throated sparrow. Here, caused by a fissure or narrow fault in the bedrock, a miracle of aspen filed as straight and precisely as if a farmer had planted a fencerow. Or here, three miniature cedars cluster where a small sink gives purchase to roots that thirst one minute, drown the next—for any weather is extreme on this surface; rain does not sink in, but gathers and floods, drought follows too quickly because the soil dries like shears. The seesaw nature of harsh seasons means that nothing grows tall. All is small, gnarled, brave. And through these short and short-lived grasslands, a rare sampler meadows the harshness. Here, arid prairie vegetation—dropseed, hairgrass, and the tiny bells of blue Prairie Smoke (an immigrant from the heartland plains!) mix roots with spike rush and swamp sedges that will drop their seeds only in near-flood conditions. They live in the extremes—albeit with some trouble.

Is this how the world survives? Always with some trouble?

Is this a lesson for my old unease? What kind of trouble is mine compared to the eons represented here. Here the short-lived plants, whose seeds have been blown in from ecosystems half a continent away, adapt and endure. Despite trouble, they root, grow, and some of their seeds, in keeping with the laws of change and mutation, survive better than others. No news there. But in the context of my reflections, I take note. To endure is to change according to the extremes, to find a notch in the rock, to make beauty among the grasses and the sparse forest. Rocks from head- to boulder-size rise up in arrangements marked by such careful spacing they are reminiscent of Japanese gardens, where the singular shape and deliberate placement of a stone makes meaning and offers the visitor the opportunity to reflect on time. Here in this wild place, I recognize a quality of deliberation—which is magically accidental.

How the heck does this happen?

I veer onto a small path that leads to a single rock composed beneath two elderly cottonwoods, leaves rustling their dry chant. I startle a thrush scrubbing at the base of the rock. I study how the rock rests . . . on the rock. Oh. These rocks, large and small, look deliberately placed because they do not sink into the earth as they would on farm land; instead they "float" individually on a bedrock plate that may have once been the bottom of the sea, surrounded by waves of short grasses, ornamented with the occasional bird. Nature making art? Or me, seeing nature through the eyes of the artist, assigning order and meaning to the random?

Here is revealed not the artist's clay transformed into vessels as Skip showed me, but the wisdom of the old sea dressed up in the seduction of thin soils, in plants and rare flowers upright and stalwart—thin earth supporting a survivor's garden. This delicate and diverse ecosystem makes meaning because it endures in a place that is so hard, because its shape and design offer contemplative order—an irony in the face of nature's messiness—that is pleasing to the brain, teasing with, what is it . . . hope?

I lift my head to the wind.

Is that a bear?

The bear—yes, it is a bear—is shuffling in my direction. It is a large black bear in no hurry, trundling over the grasslands, a mass of furry power. She stops, sniffs the air. The bear sees me, gives pause and sways her head, and though she is distant, I am suddenly grateful that this hard, dry surface provides sure footing at a dead run. I turn and make quick time for the car. I slam the door and rev the Mazda's old engine. Justifiably, the bear loses interest in the middle-aged dreamer in a ridiculous summer dress and sandals. She shambles into the ancient scrub, but her presence is warning enough that I have drifted from the necessary world and need to head back to it, to the ferry, the mainland, my next library.

But the island is not finished with me. As I am leaving the alvar, just before the woods take me in again, a sandhill crane. When I slow the car to a stop, he does not fly, but turns his dark eye to watch me for long moments, his red eye-patches giving the impression of the overtired professorial poet. His is the calm regalness of tall birds who have flown thousands of miles. We stare at each other until, with an aloof, superior expression, he turns away, struts west in his prehistoric gait. It comforts me—his balance and far-seeing demeanor—so unlike my short-sighted opinions and visions. Though I have not gained the long view of the sandhill crane, this meditation on the alvar will stay with me like a poem, the lines read from a sheet of stone.

After looking at a tall bird, after seeing a bear, after having walked a place on this planet so ancient and alive that for a moment time shifted in me, I miss David terribly. I sense the here and now, its immediate, paradoxical importance, and in the face of that and what comes next, I need my lover.

V. STEPHENSON

Back on track on the mainland U.P., the highway riding under my old tires, I roll down the windows and let my hair tangle for a while. The old Mazda swallows the miles west through Epoufette, Naubinway, Gulliver, Manistique all the way past Escanaba. I cruise over two-laners appointed with moose warnings, through mixed woods and open country that looks, even in the flush of June, a little worn, though still green at the heart. The lupines drape their purple, lavender, white coolness along the roadside, waving soft wands over scattered beer cans, battered culverts, a deer carcass.

After a few hours, you get a sense of this peninsula. Once the timber was taken and the ore carved out, the land was farmed, but not always wisely. The soil is stony and light and often run-down. Much lies fallow. The highway sweeps quickly past boarded businesses. Homes near the shore are cared for, those at a distance not always. Except for plots of pine, the common wood lots, the great trees are gone, and the forest that remains is industrial, except for the fine parks to the north. Still, bound as it is by Lake Michigan's shoreline, the air and water here are clear, and the land deliciously lonely, not with the loneliness that hurts, but simply the loneliness that is an emptying.

Some say the Upper Peninsula should have been a part of Wisconsin, but a land trade for the silver, iron, and copper gave Toledo to Ohio and the U.P. to Lansing. I can see why the Wisconsin connection persists. In Menominee County, untilled pasture gives way to long reaches of farmland. Here, the rockiness and fallow acres shift to rolling hills thick with topsoil. It is a region of farms and, located only a few miles from Wisconsin's dairy-hefted borders, most of its agriculture relates to cattle. Distant silos, gnomons of corn culture, anchor the barns and thrust up into the hazy sky over fields and pasture plotted on the obsessive 40-to-160-acre grid. Another hour west past Escanaba on U.S. 41, past Powers, into the next time zone, then south to Carney and Daggett and almost to our sister state of Wisconsin, the small town of Stephenson flirts with the Little Cedar River.

Stephenson's street grid runs just off parallel to the railroad, but the Cedar River breaks with order and meanders. Erickson Park sports a hole deep enough for families to swim. Children with Norse coloring play in the slow current, splashing in the river water. On the main street, heartland businesses: a craft and gift shop, hardware, realty, a grocery with flower barrels in front, and, down at the end of the main street, the Menominee County Library with a big garage in back.

I will stay at Strohls' B and B, right across from the Catholic Church parking lot. Art and Phyllis's finished basement bedroom and bath is comfortable, with a recessed window that offers a view at yard level of a street of quiet ranch-style homes with tidy lawns and carefully tended beds and groomed shrubs, interrupted occasionally by a riot of peonies. Art and Phyllis are solicitous—*if I should need anything, if they can be of help, and do come up for breakfast before you leave in the morning*. I've always loved it when, on any of my travels, I am not placed in the standard hotel room. I love it when Phyllis asks if they can take a picture, and they set up the camera with a shutter delay so that they can both appear with me—*so we can remember you were here—*

"We get forgetful, but if we see the picture, you'll come back to us," Phyllis says. And it is this gesture, of wanting to remember me even though it is unlikely I will return, that runs another line of connection. I imagine them looking through the album of guests, recalling as though they were singing an old hymn, each guest another verse. Here's the verse about the couple from Detroit, the one about the kids from Manistique headed for Green Bay, that writer who didn't like to stay in motels though there's a perfectly good Motel 6 right down the road. A hymn of pictures that helps define their lives.

An hour later, three Friends of the Library—Ann, Ruth, Gerri, and Carolyn—pick me up for dinner. We leave town, drive miles out on roads that divide wide fields where the scent of hay wafts even into the air-conditioned car. The eatery, Belgium Town, a bar and grill inspired by barns, rises abruptly from the surrounding acres of alfalfa and clover. I tell them my own ancestry includes the Belgians on my mother's side, and they nod, *You'd be right at home here*. When I climb out of the luxurious car, the odor of manure kicks up from the nearby farms. It does not offend me; my mother always said that smell meant everything was working.

Inside the bar we belly up to the high tables, and I order my first wine of the week, grateful for their generosity. These women are what my David calls "good folks." In any given moment, they will do the right thing. Their faces are calm, and their opinions are held mostly in courteous check. They are committed to their communities. If they are haunted, as I am, by the larger issues of the land, they do not say.

They ask about my writing, but the conversation is surface, left within the boundaries of politeness. How can I explain my writing? How can I know them? Their wish to make me feel comfortable is balanced by their desire to neither pry nor reveal too much of their own personal lives. I understand only because they are people like my people. They look out for each other, keep the peace, work hard, probably attend church, but if any shadow hangs over their histories, they do not talk about it with strangers. They contain both great steadiness and salt-of-the-earth values, though the downside is a certain stiffness, a low-level distrust of the outsider.

But I would never know that from our conversation, only from my own past. In small towns, cultural privacy surrounds like an invisible cloak. During this dinner, these women are kind and personable, and they tell me small things, how they shop in Wisconsin, how it will get dark early because we are at the far eastern edge of the central time zone. I tell them that knowing it will get dark early makes me feel lonely. One nods knowingly, one looks at me oddly, one smiles and says kindly, *"You must be tired."* And I look down at my wine, and I realize that I am like them in that I might have the same reaction to such a strange remark, but that I am different from them simply because the remark slipped out, authentic and unpredictable. For a moment I had forgotten the rules.

This time, it is not about the building that sits on the side of a street, attached to a school, not about the sweet reading room where a table and chairs and people are already waiting. Nor is it the reading itself. This time it is about the garage and the woman named Ann, who shows me what a library can be in a community so widespread that people cannot easily get to the library.

"Do you want to see the bookmobile?" she asks shyly.

The bookmobile?

In her pretty dress, her graying hair coiling down her back, she leads me through a maze of rooms to the rear of the building, through a wide door and into the garage. We stand on a cement landing and look down into the large bay. There it is, a gleaming, trailer-style, on-road library. She smiles, and we look at each other, recognizing the secret, obsessive pleasure, *Oh, there are books in there!* She unlocks the door, turns on the power, and for the second time on this trip, I step into a trailer remodeled for a purpose other than living, this one a traveling library. Loaded with books.

Bright lights and big colors. The interior is a people-sized shoebox lined with titles from kiddy lit to mysteries, from best sellers to histories, from cookbooks to computers. It is a crowded, vital portable library.

"I drive it myself." Her shyness cannot quite cover her pride.

She rolls out several times a week and travels Menominee County highways to schools, villages, the parking lot of the single business that may keep a town name alive. She has loaned books in used-car and church lots, playgrounds and farmyards. I look at her face. A clear pleasure rises in her as she speaks of people who come to the bookmobile, especially the children who come—and she tells me that the bookmobile assists literacy. She smiles widely speaking of the booted men and the hefty women, the children with grubby hands. *Oh, they come here for how-to's and stuff, but here they can just read something, not for a purpose but just to enjoy it.* Here is the moment, here in the farmland of working folks, a commitment to driving a library to people so they may also have the pleasure of books.

She tells me about a boy who taught himself to read better. She tells me that whenever the bookmobile came to his town, he spent as much of the day as he could picking out books and reading to her slowly and quietly whenever she was not with other borrowers. I see the boy in my mind, his plain face, his intent eyes focused as he turns page after page, the mouth—is it dirty, smeared with mustard or peanut butter?—forming the words for her in his chair in this place that will arrive like some magic creature and then leave again.

And in its wake there are books.

Bookmobiles are familiar, have been around long enough that they have become a quaint rendering of the concept of free knowledge that underpins the American readership. But in the context of my travels, my own renewed sensibility about libraries and the Michigan places I have visited, the bookmobile here takes on that resonance of something newly discovered. Books on wheels, words on miles, the ever-turning journey of language—all of it packed up into a self-propelled contraption. A trailer on the trail of the imagination. Perhaps it is pure projection that I feel more fondness for this revamped motor home than I have toward any of the rooted libraries on this expedition because I, too, am traveling. The bookmobile is a traveling place. I, in my rusted-out Mazda, am in a traveling place, carrying not only my books, but the interior volumes of my restless mind, my heart—both wayward and homeward by turns. This library tour has taken my books to new places, but as much as that, it has taken my thinking to new places and has gotten me out of my bookish nerd-head and asked me to move around, see something new—or something very old but new to me. It has made me park, literally and figuratively, in places I would not have parked. It has not eased my dis-ease, but it has put me firmly into this place, this Michigan.

I would like to say we stole the keys, climbed in, backed its blocky body out of its berth and took the bookmobile for a long spin, testing its mettle and wheel base. I'd like to say that we took on the miles, a regional writer and a reference librarian, ever after known down at the swimming hole as those *crazy women what stole that trailer of books,* that we ran the countryside, barnyards, grain fields, the two-tracks and back roads, bridges and ditches, that we scattered books and ideas and thinking and the pleasure of a story all over these counties before we hit the Wisconsin line. I would like to say we didn't stop, but headed out "for the territories" as Huck Finn would have said, that we just kept going, as Thelma and Louise might have, that we dreamed ourselves and our portable library into a new world where we knew what to do with the sadness and worry of our times. I would like to say that as we rolled along we changed this not perfect, not mad world.

But for me it would most likely be the other way around. It would change me. The romps of mind on an imagined hostage bookmobile are one way to escape and heal from the "weight of the world." But they are inspired by the real places like Stephenson, like an island that opens to eons, and like people who anchor me in my own past, who remember me though I may not return. I drive highways that tell me who I am in the language of rock and water, that offer me a slice of citizenry in this Michigan, in this America, in this place where I have the freedom of the road as well as the road's imagined journey.

As it is, I spend so much time in the bookmobile, fingering Ann's selections, listening to stories of her books and her people, that I am nearly late for the reading and have to dash back to the reading room, where I stand before the lively crowd of twenty. I thank Ann first. People nod and turn. She seems surprised and smiles, and it is she who brings cookies to me afterward, the simple gesture of gratitude. I read the tractor story as well as I have the entire trip—and the memory rings as it should, of how the old Allis Chalmers, for good or ill, taught me both motion and power. My first answer to the questions of restlessness. I cannot speak for these people, for the kind women who took me to dinner. Here in this June farm country, among ordinary and extraordinary people, amidst popular and sacred books housed in both building and vehicle, I am defined not by essence or contrast, but by both place and motion, the need for home coupled with the tug away.

VI. INDIAN RIVER

Back to the Lower Peninsula, to Indian River, my last reading, mid-afternoon in a lovely new building just three hours from home. Now, I really am tired, and even the lively librarian, Cindy Lou Poquette, and the sweet Friends cannot quite cheer me. The bright spirit that touched me in Stephenson has been dulled by too many hours in the car and too many days away from David, who roots me in the place called home. I put on the good face, *So glad to be here, and what a lovely day,* and follow

the good-author protocol, but the afternoon reading does not
draw. Besides the Friends, only two other people show up. I
give a solid, if not stellar reading. I sell three books.

They do offer me cookies, and gratefully, for the last time, I
pack them up *for the road*.

But on the way out of town, I remember the cross and turn
back, catch the side road. Indian River is the site of The Cross
in the Woods Shrine, one the largest crucifixes in the world,
a fifty-five-foot crucifix made of a single redwood. I haven't
seen it since I was a child. I remember an impressive moment
when I was a little girl and my family made the trek to Mass
here. My mother teared up, and both my parents were deeply
moved, while my brothers, wildly excited by an outdoor
church, crawled on the grass under the benches that served as
pews. I remember staring at the cross, being a little frightened
by the enormous corpus, and then pulling inside myself and
not feeling anything except that it was big, just too big to take
in. I don't think my imagination had evolved enough to understand that the largeness was symbolic. I hadn't yet gotten to
metaphor.

The crucifix remains powerfully dominant in the landscape,
still massive, solid and enduring, the corpus some thirty-one
feet high by twenty-two feet wide. The grain of the wood
is lost now, not the dark grain I saw as a child, because the
cross has been painted at the request of the sculptor, Marshall
Frederick. In the congregational space, the pews have been
upgraded, a tidy berm with summer annuals slopes to the al-
tar, and behind it, the cross looms over the highest trees, sil-
houetted by a moody Michigan sky. Along the side, the Scala
Santa, a stairway where pilgrims kneel and rise and kneel again
as they pray their way up the twenty-eight steps, replicating
the steps the Christ was supposed to have taken to his Gol-

gotha. Once at the top, they may touch the base of the cross. From directly beneath, they look up and see the feet and head of the Christ in a distorted perspective.

I am not so devout. After meandering the smaller shrines on the side paths, I find my way around to the back of the artificial hill on which this giant symbol is planted. Here, the grass is lanky with sedge and knapweed. I discover a set of older wooden steps with a wobbly two-by-four railing, probably for maintenance people. It is these steps I climb to touch the cross, coming up behind it, not out of any assumed humility, but because I still don't like to look at the corpus—it seems overrated, this contemplation of suffering. Perhaps that is what frightened me as a child, the contemplation of suffering. But I do pray—though my form of prayer has always been more like thinking toward . . . what? Water, stone, land? A place beyond—or is it inside—me?

In keeping with the ritual, on each of these steps I stop for a moment. I think about the world, this American freedom of being able to travel, to just go. I think about Skip, about people who support human expression. I think about the people who gave me a place to stay and about people reading enough so that real knowledge will be gained. I think, with immense gratitude, about the librarians: Kathleen, Peggi, Pat, Joy, Cindy Lou, Ann. I think about the bookmobile and the listeners. I think about how we might make a better world. Finally I breathe a prayer, or as close as I come, that my writing might somehow do some good.

At the top step, I look up, and because I stand behind the cross, I can see little of the sculpture. My eyes follow the straight lines of the post to the cross beam and what I see at this angle is a distorted crossroads. Like X marks the spot, tipped to its side. How many Michigan and U.S. highways, gravel turnoffs, two-tracks, even the scraped-clean bedrock of the alvar, have I crossed on this trip? And I think about the crossroads not only as the place where one turns off or goes straight, but as the coming-together place, like Four Corners in Drummond.

I am in that crossroads place.

I have traveled in a state where good things happened, where people seemed able to love their places, where the sadness that feels inevitable is held in abeyance by stories and listening, by reading and being read to, in all its guises. By libraries. Though simple, this is not a balm. I cannot speak for everyone, but I suspect, like so many citizens, we as a nation are on our own spiritual road trip. I know the road we face is immensely complicated, that freedoms are bound to responsibilities, that we are a people of often terrifying contradiction, that in the course of our history we have made and remade our places, not always for the good, and only recently have we come to think of saving them. And now there is some question as to whether or not we can. But in this moment, here is the small comfort, a balm of sorts that doesn't negate the larger picture, but offers some consolation. My America may still be found in the almost invisible goodnesses of place within place, in the spirit places within real places, in the surprise of a Michigan road when the turn off leads to a new lake or meadow or bookmobile where there just may be the kernel of a story that just might take flight. Perhaps it is that, the gift of imagination that I feel in this moment, the freedom to make up a better ending, that is my final comfort. I don't know what my own journey means yet—but I suspect it will go on making meaning for a while, that this trip will stare at me like a sandhill crane, and I will continue to read it as it has read me.

But now, I have only a short way to go before I arrive at my coming-together place, where the four corners of love, mind, body, and home locate their coordinates both on the interior map and the real place where David waits with his warm and open arms.

Heart of Sand

Sleeping Bear Dunes National Lakeshore, Michigan

Before the legend of the Sleeping Bear became Michigan's state story, I was struck by its sad contradictions. It is the tale of the great she-bear, Michimokwa, who, to escape a Wisconsin forest fire, swam with her cubs across Lake Michigan to a new peninsula. Though she reached the open sand on the Michigan side, her young cubs drowned a short way from the Michigan shore.

In the story, the great spirit, Gitche Manitou, transformed the cubs into the two islands we call the Manitous, but it is that west-facing dune on the shore that is the pivot point for the legend, the one that represents the great she-bear watching those two islands. She is said to watch from the dunes for her cubs to make it to shore. She is said to call for them. She is said to sleep in peace under the sand. I know how stories twist, how they must mean many things in order to last, but how could she sleep in peace and be ever watchful at the same time?

Would I understand it better if I went there?

In the autumn, I decide to visit Sleeping Bear Dunes National Lakeshore and walk to the Sleeping Bear, the single dune identified by sailors among the seventy thousand acres of dune and forest and islands that are named for her. I decide to go on my birthday, to mark the moment with a look at the great mother.

I drive the park's forested scenic road to the point where it opens to the light and sand of the dunes. I park, hike the boardwalk to a lookout with benches offering a view of the Bear to the north. This civilized platform is where most people stop, read the story printed on the signs, and then return to their cars. From here I can see the rough rise and darkness of the dune in the distance.

A mile? Two?

Cold and bluster bully me as I squeeze under the railings and step off the lookout, cutting directly across the dunes, trudging through this northern desert. From the lookout, the dune seemed close enough, but when I leave the deck and start walking through sand so soft it leaves a clean print only after rain, I realize there is a good reason not many people visit the specific dune I have chosen. The hard walk up and down the crumbling slopes dampens my determination to find a place I have never been.

But it is my birthday.

I stumble along the shoreline bluff, walking slowly through varied soil, sometimes soft sand, sometimes course gravel or crusty silt—all of it light. The wind gusts fiercely along these bluffs, and even though the dunes are still snowless, winter is already pushing its way toward these arid places. As I move over the drifts of glacial debris, walking absorbs my attention. I watch my feet, notice snail shells in abundance, along with small stony fossils. Here and there are scattered rust-colored beer cans leftover from the days when the dunes were privately owned and dune buggies carrying thrill-seekers tore across the fragile dune ecosystem. There are tracks everywhere in this part of the dunes—deer, raccoon, mice, gulls and small birds—though I see no animals and hear little except the alarm of the crows, the distant roar of waves below the bluffs. The wind picks up, slams sand against my jeans.

I think I may be lost.

Deep swales. I cannot see the lake or the distant reference point of the dune. I stop, disoriented, pull my hood back to let the wind cool my face, and then start again, but without a clear sense of direction. I am out here alone, and even my husband does not know I have decided on this birthday sojourn. I wonder if I have lost my bearings and study the slopes for landmarks. Just as I think I should turn back before my tracks are obliterated by wind, a slow rise carries me up a low ridge and there, across the distance, high green foliage marking the Bear. I keep going, fighting wind and poor footing and now, colder air.

Half an hour later, having spanned the final mile and struggled up through rough scrub, I crest the rim—gasping for breath, and look down into what is the bowl of the bear. I had expected something else, a plateau marked with thick and tattered shrubbery. But this dune is deceptive, secretive. What from a distance looks like a hilltop and rises like a rough upturned dish, like some solid and long-standing pedernal, is instead something in motion. Open space. Instead of the flat-topped mound that would have been the geological metaphor for the bear, a hollow. The Bear is a huge basin, winnowed out and cast empty by wind, an immense sink of sand.

It has become a blowout.

A blowout is a dune summit or ridge that may have once looked like a lush foliage-covered hilltop. But because of the lightness and fragility of the soil—almost dust—and the death, due to drought or other weather conditions, of that vegetation, plus exposure to the constant westerlies, the dune sand erodes away from the roots, especially at the crest of these hills. After years of enduring this relentless wind, the vegetation blows away, and the dune begins to hollow itself out, like a bowl, weathered down from the high point, leaving the lower, less exposed sides to rise like a rim. Dune walkers commonly stumble on blowouts all over the open duneland, but this one is startling for its immensity and grandeur, a huge basin carved by wind.

And then, there is the beauty of her bones.

From that crater of sand where her body would have rested, ghost trees rise, scattered and leaning and awful. The remnants of this spirit forest are scattered like ribs and femurs and spine. They shimmer silver gray, smoothed by the gales, their grain polished to gleam against the half-lit day.

I stand there for a long time, asking quietly if I may enter, and when the wind drops, I take it as acceptance and climb inside, where the wind drops but never ceases.

How long can one explore a void? The inside of the word *hollow*? I wander, spiraling lower, touching the driftwood trees that were once green and are now an uncanny architecture, shards of some immense being. I sniff cold air, dryness, dune dust. Wind mutes and huffs through this place, and over the years, it has not only hollowed the bowl but shaped a broad opening at the west side of the blowout—as though the sand that once made the mound was poured out of a wide spigot. But this is the opposite of the truth. The broad opening is where the constant westerlies enter the blowout and lift sand particles up and carry them east and farther into the dunes— shifting the landscape every season.

Finally, I do what I have been avoiding. There is here a place within a place. I look to the center of the blowout, which contains a smaller mound, still intact, around which the wind has worked all these years. It is perhaps two stories high, and despite the fact that all else around it is hollowed out and left to bones, it stands over this desert and the skeletal trees, a rough, grass-pocked cone with its top sheered off. I have been circling its irregular slopes cautiously because I feel the anomaly. This entire rise has been blown away, but this core has remained, grasses still clinging to its surface. I choose the least steep slope on the backside, the slope protected from the lake winds, and scramble up, slipping with every step. Finally I am perched on this upturned funnel in the middle of windy emptiness. Breathless, I lie down and watch the rush of combed skies.

Is this place within a place what's left of her mammoth heart? Is this heart of sand the stalwart core of emptiness? It is a place that simply resists. Resists just enough to hold, even against the force of the west winds. Resists a bit longer than the rest of the earth against the inevitable wearing down. A symbol of the Bear, who waits—held in the paradox of eternal sleep and eternal watchfulness—for her cubs, those distant islands of Manitou.

Before I climbed the interior mound, I had been imagining that her bones would someday rise and gather themselves into body, whole and muscled and covered with the mat of her great hide. I saw her walk on water, raise up her startled cubs, cuff them into motion, and then lumber over the land to call us all out of sleep. This is how I hoped the legend would wake us, wake me. As something fierce and alive, resurrected in power. But now, sitting on the mound, staring out, I imagine her heart defined by a will to stay, to endure a little longer the inevitable winds.

What does a thousand years mean to a mother waiting?

Since then, I have tried to make the trek once a year, usually in the fall when the isolation is more remarkable. I know better ways to get there now. I have learned to go quietly, with reverence, and not to move anything, not to touch much. I always climb the mound, sit in what I perceive as the center of not just this dune, but of all the shifting acres for miles around.

I have come to love the wind here, the power it has to erase through its insistent presence. Just as it has blown out the hilltop, the very place that represented the great mother, Michimokwa, the wind has fragmented the story itself, altered what the place means. The meaning shifts, catches in the wind, lifts and transforms until there will be nothing left of even her heart. This is not sad, but rather the wind waking the imagination and simultaneously, paradoxically, waking us to emptiness, to the limits of story. To mystery. This is the wind making the place where story meets void, the opposite of meaning. The hollow bowl that also shapes our being.